Questions and Answers for Deep South Gardeners

Nellie Neal

&

B. B. Mackey Books
P. O. Box 475
Wayne, Pennsylvania, 19087
www.mackeybooks.com

1

Questions and Answers for Deep South Gardeners

~~~~~~~~~~~~~~~~~~~~~

To my husband Dave, who believed.

~~~~~~~~~~~~~~~~~~~~~

Books may be ordered from any full service bookstore, from www.amazon.com, or by mail from **B. B. Mackey Books, P.O. Box 475, Wayne, PA 19087-0475** *Or use our website with shopping cart at http://www.mackeybooks.com.*

A Cutting Garden for Florida, Third Edition. Betty Mackey and Monica Moran Brandies. Revised 2001. Grow flowers for bouquets in your Florida landscape. $15.95, paperbound. ISBN 09616338-2-4.

Herbs and Spices for Florida Gardens. Monica Moran Brandies. Floridians, grow herbs for flavor, health, beauty, crafts, scent, and garden color. 1996. $15.50, paperbound. ISBN 09616338-6-7.

Florida Gardening: The Newcomer's Survival Manual. Monica Moran Brandies. Laugh off the garden perils and grow a wonderful new landscape. 1993. $9.95, paperbound. 6th printing. ISBN 09616338-3-2.

Bless You For the Gifts. Monica Moran Brandies. True stories of life in a large, rural family, written with warmth and humor. 1997. $10.95, paperbound. ISBN 09616338-7-5.

Creating and Planting Garden Troughs. Joyce Fingerut and Rex Murfitt. The complete guide to creating and planting wonderful, lighter-weight garden troughs. A winner of the American Horticultural Society's Year 2000 Book Award. Praise-filled reviews. $21.00. Hardcover, 7 x 10 inches. Color photos, 170 pages, index, resource list, bibliography. ISBN 1-8934430-0-0.

In Another Light. Lucy Fuchs. Gentle yet piercing poetry, elegant and accomplished. 2002. Some of the poems were published previously but most are new. $8.95. 36 pages. Comb-bound. ISBN 18934430-5-1

Garden Notes Through the Years. Organize your garden records with this four-year blank journal designed by Betty Mackey, 1994. $11.95, paperbound, comb binding. ISBN 09616338-4-0.

The Plant Collector's Notebook. Blank notebook for tracking garden plants, designed by Betty Mackey, revised 1997. $7.95, paperbound, comb binding. ISBN 09616338-5-9.

Garden Days. Betty Mackey. For any year of YOUR garden notes. 5" x 8.5" journal with week-by-week layout. Record bloom times, plant names, bird and wildlife observations, and more. $7.95. 120 pages, comb-bound. Red poppy cover design. ISBN 1-893443035.

A Cutting Garden for California. Pat Kite and Betty Mackey. 1990. How to grow flowers for bouquets at home in your California landscape. $8.00, paperbound. ISBN 09616338-1-6.

Questions and Answers for Deep South Gardeners. Nellie Neal, Mississippi call-in radio host (SuperTalk MS). Got questions? Here's the unbeatable answer book, and it's lots of fun to read. $12.95, paperbound, illustrated, and indexed. ISBN 1-893443-06-X.

Postage is free on any two or more books. See last page for order form. Add $2.00 postage on orders of one book only. Pennsylvania residents only, please add 6% state sales tax.

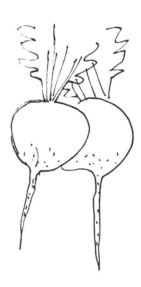

Foreword

Listening inspires me and this book is the result. I was a shy child who dug my chin into my chest when asked a question. But my silence was full of inner sound and I remember replaying conversations I'd witnessed, imagining what I would have said if only I could have. Speech and drama classes taught me to use what I'd gleaned from listening, and I have been speaking up ever since. I still spend a great deal of time listening, especially to the gardeners whose questions fill this book.

 I believe that to garden is to develop a rhythm that nurtures both plant and grower. When I am able to spend even an hour each day in the garden, I find a comfortable groove that keeps my knees flexible, and my plants healthy. My approach to gardening is simple: start with the dirt and stay with the program. That is, amend native soil as needed to create good growing conditions, then make smart plant and site choices, provide the water and fertilizer required, and keep an eye out for pests so you can head them off. It's that simple, and that complicated. I trust you will find plenty of details in these pages.

In a lifetime of gardening (over thirty years professionally) I have learned from growers of every stripe: my grandfather, the vegetable guru; university professors at LSU where I studied horticulture as a graduate student; fellow garden writers and Master Gardeners; friends in the field; and neighbors who, among them, can grow anything. All have a common path, if different means, to their gardening ends. Most have a deep devotion to one plant or another, but I don't—I'll try to grow anything once. I am not a rosarian although I do grow roses, and I'll plant any flower I can find, regardless of what it's called or where it grew originally. I don't claim expertise in turf, but have grown beautiful lawns. Vegetables aren't my exclusive passion yet every year I have tomatoes to give away. And I've been know to spend inordinate amounts of time tending plants people give me, resulting in a truly odd collection. Currently among the plants that found me are a camellia gift from a plant society, an assortment of night-blooming cereus whose owner had to move, two Norfolk pines my friends tried to kill, and a nice bed of asparagus that beat the bulldozer— all doing fine, thank you. I pride myself on having incessant curiosity about plants, and on being a generalist in these times when everyone else seems to be a specialist.

I could not write without the teachers who filled my mind with the scientific method, teaching me to ferret out the bunk and recognize the real deal in research and practice. Thank you, Dr. Ed O'Rourke, for teaching me how to grow. Every now and then someone reteaches a concept to me in a way that I can finally understand. My thanks to Bob Brzuszek for

5

insights on the zen of plant siting. No editor deserves my thanks more than Lynn Ashford, especially when it comes to converting horticulturese to relevant, real world language.

I thank the callers to my radio shows, for raising my communication consciousness. Writing is a disciplined vocation, and I thank my parents for whatever discipline I possess. It is not inborn in me. Thanks, too, to my colleagues in the Garden Writers Association who conspire to improve my writing and focus.

Special thanks to my family, for so much joy, and for understanding the value of take-out Chinese food in the life of a freelance writer. Last but not least, thanks to G-d, for giving me life in America.

Introduction

As one described by my own mother as 'stranger than fiction' (at worst) and 'offbeat' (at best), I abhor labels that stereotype people. However we try to categorize them, people who grow plants resist classification and I applaud that. So I'm not willing or able to say that this book is for 'novice' or 'veteran' gardeners since nearly every one I've ever met was a bit of both. But I sincerely think all but true plant snobs (those who mistake species micromanagement for gardening) will find something in here of value. Maybe you'll get a question of your own answered, but in addition to specific information I hope to pass along a sense of how interrelated growing different kinds of plants can be and what it's really like to garden twelve months a year.

The questions in this book come from gardeners in the southeastern United States and are applicable to other parts of the country with similar growing seasons —East Texas down to the Gulf, across the breadth of the Southeast to the lower Atlantic coast, and southern and coastal California. Although conditions on a given day in Memphis can be quite different on the same day in Pensacola, the issues gardeners face in both places are much the same: we may set out tomato plants a week or two apart, but still weeks before it is the season for northern gardeners to do so.

I will refer occasionally to south, deep south, and deeper south conditions and ranges of plants—these catchall terms refer to the areas shown on the regional map on page 10. These divisions are noteworthy, for there are times when the differences are important to gardeners, yet in many cases they are not. For example, gardeners on the Gulf Coast cannot ever count on a cold winter to reduce insect populations as the more northern zones can, in most years, but doing a fall cleanup to prevent insects overwintering is equally important in all the zones. However, it may have to be done in September in Dallas, but November in New Orleans.

I have gardened all over Mississippi, Louisiana, and California, with stints as a visiting helper in Texas, Florida, and Tennessee. In these diverse regions, we have more commonalities than differences, especially when you consider the microclimates we create with urban infrastructure and dense landscape plantings.

Challenging soil types and high humidity mean all our soils can stand improvement. Winters are considered relatively mild overall, but that only means they're unpredictable. Temperatures drop rapidly overnight, slowing plant growth, then warm up for a week or a month, stimulating them to grow again. Rainfall can fill a rain gauge in a single day, then dry up for months on end.

Our challenges are tough on all but the best suited plants. If an old plant or a new one can survive, we make it a favorite. Heat-tolerant, thunder-

storm-proof—these are the words to look for in choosing plants for the South. But plant nuts like me find ways around the conditions. For example, a plant label that says 'full sun' may not mean a full dose of southern sunshine all day long. The plant gets pale, wilts daily, and dies prematurely. Read labels and instructions provided by non-southern sources with a grain of salt, and remember that, here in the South, even sunlovers can use a little shade in the late afternoon.

For the most part we grow the same plants in nearly the same seasons throughout the South, but Southern seasons are subtly different from those in other parts of the country. We garden least in summer, plant tomatoes twice a year, and grow pansies in the winter: no wonder transplanted gardeners sometimes feel everything they know is upside down!

In the 'nineties, I was co-publisher of *Loose Dirt, a newsletter for southern gardeners*, and wrote its 'Chore Chart,' a collection of monthly tips for a series of plant categories (annuals, herbs and vegetables, etc.) which are adapted and expanded here. Because it was a quarterly publication, we had to divide the year up somehow, and soon it became obvious that the traditional months of the seasons didn't make sense here.

For us, here in the warmest areas of the United States, fall starts in October and lasts until the end of the calendar year. Many a December day is warm, while March is often 'the cruelest month,' cold, wet, and fatal to summer annuals planted too soon. So January, February, and March comprise winter to us, and April kicks off spring, which continues pleasantly into May and June. July, August, and September, the South's summer, are the province of the highest temperatures and the worst insect invasions.

This book is organized by the Southern seasons. Each chapter begins with an introduction to the season, as well as a longer article about essential

cultural practices and growing notes based on my own gardening life. Finally, and probably because I was an English major in undergraduate school, I have chosen several words that every gardener should know, with definitions only I could craft.

The book is carefully indexed by topic. For example, a question in spring about iris borers will be indexed both by the plant's name and the problem described. Thus, the index will direct you to this entry whether you look up iris or look up borers.

Following the garden terms (vocabulary) in each chapter, you'll find the heart of the book. Each chapter has numerous real questions asked by real gardeners who call in to talk to me on the SuperTalk MS Radio Network. I have expanded the original answers to encompass my gardening experiences in the deep, deeper, and deepest south. As indicated on the zone map (next page), the tropical south is outside the scope of this book.

You can read the book straight through, or one season at a time, or concentrate on one plant group and read the whole year's worth of that first. Or you may have a particular plant or problem and want to get my take on it, so you'll look it up in the index regardless of the season. If your attention span or available time is really short, put the book in the bathroom and read it one question at a time. I know that if this is a good book, you'll make notes in the margins, and there is room for them there. If it's really good, you'll have to give copies to your friends so they'll quit borrowing yours.

*****

ZONES

The South is a big place, and this book covers most but not all of it. Here is a map to help you understand my answers in relation to where you live and garden. Heat and humidity dominate summer weather in all zones, a little less so in some places where breezes off the ocean or a cool front lingering just over the mountains make it more tolerable, at least at night. But it's southern winters that drive gardeners crazy—it's not the 'sunny south' folks imagine. All of the zones have dreadful, bone-chilling cold days, with freezing temperatures that drive the rain and sleet right through you.

I have divided the territory into three basic zones based on a combination of traditional cold hardiness zones (USDA) and the newer information about heat quotients (AHS). The map includes areas of the United States from Texas to the Atlantic coast, and much of it is applicable to California's coastal climates as well. Gardeners in the mountainous regions in the north and west of the South and tropical areas of farthest south Florida and Texas will find that the principles apply, but my suggestions for when to do what may not.

DEEP SOUTH STATES
Zone Map

Deep South. Here, from El Paso to Little Rock, Memphis, Birmingham, Atlanta, and Raleigh, winters usually include some snow, but few nights ever fall below zero. Those who garden here claim to have the best of both worlds since they can grow both crape myrtles and Persian lilacs. In this zone you'll find that the the southern limit of some plants meets the northern limits of others, giving gardeners here a wide palette of species to grow.

Deeper South. This zone includes Dallas and a large swath of Texas, flows across Louisiana, including my hometown of Monroe, and extends through central Mississippi, Alabama, Georgia, and both Carolinas. Snow flies, conditions are too often ripe for dangerous ice storms. Wet, cold weeks give way unexpectedly to days of sunny weather often enough that plants and people get confused. Plants that need dormancy only get a brief rest some seasons, and when it turns cold suddenly, your gloves are invariably left wherever you were the day it last warmed up.

Deepest South. Corpus Christi and Houston, Baton Rouge and New Orleans, Mobile, Tallahassee, Jacksonville, and Savannah: this region offers shady live oaks and beaches with breezes to cut through summer's humid nights. But don't be fooled. It is not a tropical zone. Half hardy or tender perennials are still less than perennial in most places, and summer annuals won't grow year round by any means. A cold day here is still cold, and with more rainfall annually than other parts of the South, flooding can be a serious problem winter or summer.

10

Chapter 1
Deep South Fall
October, November, December

~~~~~~~ *Autumn in the Garden* ~~~~~~~

Autumn seems to come sooner some years than others, that first really cool spell that marks the season's change. Leaves fall by the bucket every day in October, and candelabra trees bloom right along with sasanquas. Most years, the cool spell lasts a few weeks on the heels of hurricane season, then Indian summer returns. Consensus is, fall makes for the best days to work soil, construct pergolas and decks, and, early in the season, to sod new lawns. During a typical fall day in the Deep South, if there is such a thing, daytime temperatures may reach well into the 70's, with nights dropping through the 50's and 40's, down to average first frosts between November 1 and December 10. Rainfall depends on hurricanes early and determined cold fronts later in the season, but feels cool to the touch. It's considered the best gardening season if you measure those things by the comfort of the gardener.

Trees and shrubs. Plant shrubs and trees to your heart's content from now through February for ideal transplanting conditions. Prepare the soil first everywhere you want to plant this year, so that even during a wet winter, you'll be planting while others are waiting for native soils to dry out.

Evergreen, single plant hedges are fine, but drop in one flowering shrub for every two evergreens to make that hedgerow more interesting. Prepare to transplant native seedling trees in a month or so: use a sharp shovel to dig around the trunk and send the roots toward what will be the new rootball. Go six inches out from a one-inch trunk and make sharp cuts in a solid circle around the tree now. Give it a month or more to get ready, then dig and replant the same day.

Questions and Answers for Deep South Gardeners

Herbs and vegetables. Make a bed now for January plantings of potatoes, English peas, snowpeas, and onions. Dump in some leaves as you rake them, an inch of composted manure, a bit of ground bark, and a dusting of lime. Till or dig in well, then shop for seeds. Look for short-season varieties that will be ready to eat well before the weather gets warm.

Perennial Herbs
For Garden Or Container Culture

1. chives (*Allium schoenoprasum*, onion chives,

   and *A. tuberosum*, garlic chives)
2. lemon balm (*Melissa officinalis*)
3. mint (*Mentha spp.*)
4. winter savory (*Santureja montana*)
5. thyme (*Thymus vulgaris*)
6. Mexican mint marigold (*Tagetes lucida*) for tarragon flavor
7. oregano (*Origanum spp.*)
8. sage (*Salvia officinalis*)
9. rosemary (*Rosemarinus officinalis*)
10. bay (*Laurus nobilis*)

Start planting leaf lettuces like 'Red Sails' and 'Black-seeded Simpson', and greens from collards to mustard and swiss chard. Plant weekly to extend the season, and don't forget the mesclun—that's the mixture sold for big bucks all winter as spring greens. Lettuce (and carrots, too) need light to sprout, so press them into the soil, don't bury them.

Harvest broccoli while the flowerheads are tight and green—don't let the yellow flowers emerge or the broc will be bitter. Leave the plants where they are and look for delicious side shoots to continue the harvest.

Herbs to plant in fall include annuals parsley, cilantro, garlic, fennel, and dill, to suit their preference for cooler growing conditions. Plant rosemary, thyme, and other perennial herbs, too, in beds or containers. Add herbs to traditional ornamental plantings. Use parsley and pansies for an edible annual border, and add rosemary to shrub and perennial beds. Its gray leaves and blue flowers make a great complement to favorites like lantana and St. John's wort.

Annual flowers and vines. Plant pansies early this season, but seek alternatives if the varieties available in your area have flopped in wet weather. Calendula can be sturdier, snapdragons just as colorful. *Viola tricolor,* or Johnny jump-up, isn't just a prolific reseeder to avoid. Improved varieties like 'Sorbet' are resilient after storms with bicolor blooms for months.

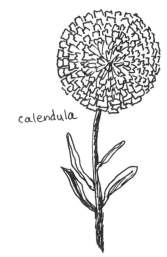
calendula

Harvest the hard fruits of 'tater vine (aka monkey balls, but botanically *Discorea bulbifera*) once the leaves have fallen. Store them dry for planting in the spring. If you don't have this tough, sunloving, shade-producing, heart-shaped vine, find somebody who does and get some. Drop a piece of lattice over four 4-by-4 poles sunk for corners, then plant 'tater vines at the corners—voila, instant shade. Next fall the balls will hang for easy picking.

Ornamental cabbages and kales can look like someone shot holes the size of a pencil right through the leaves. At the first sign, dust the plants with dipel (*Bacillus thuringiensis*, a natural predator of the cabbageworms invading your plants).

Perennial flowers and vines. Vines that bloom for months, like coral honeysuckle (*Lonicera sempervirens* 'Cedar Lane') can be pruned lightly just to train and contain the vines, or more severely to rejuvenate them. If leaf miners or other insects have been a problem, use oil spray now to cut down their population next summer.

Perennials For Shady Gardens

1. southern shield, hollyleaf, maidenhair, and other hardy ferns.
2. plantain lily (Hosta fortunei 'Albomarginata' and others)
3. wild blue phlox (Phlox divaricata)
4. Indian pink (Spigelia marilandica)
5. purple heart (Setcreasea pallida)
6. woods violets (viola odora)
7. butterfly lily (Hedychium coronarium)
8. cardinal flower (Lobelia cardinalis)
9. cast iron plant (Aspidistra elatior)
10. Lenten rose (Helleborous orientalis)

Put perennials to bed as they go dormant—look for tan to brown leaves and stems. Cut stems down almost (but not quite) to the crown or ground, then mulch with a thin layer of compost topped with fresh raked leaves, ground bark, or pine straw. Don't cover the crown completely! In late fall, cut back and mulch lantana and butterfly bushes even if they haven't lost a leaf yet, to promote overall plant health.

Plant divisions or offsets of perennials so that you are grouping those with similar growth habits, or the bullies will run over the more sedate types. And put the bog plants like cardinal flower (*Lobelia cardinalis*) where you'll remember to water in dry times. Newly planted perennials need to be watered deeply, but not often for their first year to encourage deep rooting and long life. Two to three times a month should do.

Bulbs. Start forcing paperwhite narcissus for holiday gifts and decorating. Nestle the bulbs, don't bury them, in pots filled with marble chips or gravel. Water once and put the pots in a dark place—under the sink in the bathroom is handy. Water sparingly until the white new growth is about four inches tall. This controls their ultimate height. Take them out and grow them on in a sunny window.

If beds of naturalized bulbs like daffodils didn't bloom well last year, fertilize early this season with bulb food. But, if all you get this year is green, plan to divide them once the leaves die down next summer.

Keep tender bulbs (and bulblike roots) like dahlia and caladium dry over the winter and prevent them from freezing. Store the clean bulbs in cedar shavings, peat moss, pine needles, or other material in a way that keeps their sides from touching each other. Mesh bags or old pantyhose work well to contain the bulbs and provide good air circulation in storage.

Groundcovers and lawns. Some folks lime the lawn every three years, or six, or never, but you won't know for sure if and when the soil needs 'sweetening' unless you test. Kits are available commercially and from extension services in every state. To cut down on inhaling dust, choose pelletized lime products.

Consider overseeding lawns with perennial ryegrass—think of it as a cozy blanket for the precious sod. Ryegrass helps prevent erosion and wind damage, looks lovely all winter, and mowing it a few times provides important green matter for the compost pile.

Mulch and weed between established plants of the groundcovers you're encouraging to grow together. Divide clumps of liriope and mondo grass and replant them right away. Instead of planting clumps in martial rows to edge a border, set the plants in a zigzag (staggered) pattern, and pick a few spots to thicken their stand. The result will be neat looking, but softer and more welcoming.

Fruit. Leave muscadine vines and blueberry bushes alone. Enjoy their fall colors, then rake up fallen leaves to prevent overwintering insects and diseases.

Mulch figs deeply, but don't smother the young trunks of other fruits. It's true that winter winds and temperatures can dehydrate new plantings, whether you're growing grapevines or plums. Wrap those thin-skinned trunks with burlap strips if their site and conditions will dry them out.

Slightly acid, well-drained native soils are ideal for nonastringent (sweet and crisp fruited) persimmons. More exotic flavors will be found in the puckering type (astringent) but they can be more fickle to grow. Check to see if the variety you like the looks and taste of needs a pollinator, then plant both.

Plants in pots. Bring holiday cacti (Thanksgiving and Christmas types) indoors before nights fall into the forty-degree range. Slip their pots into

decorated baskets, but slip them off again for watering so it pours on through. Never let pots sit in saucers full of irrigation water—they'll suffer if they take it back up into the soil.

Go beyond pansies for porch and patio planters. Drop in a small shrub: dwarf barberry for red color or holly for berries. Surround it with little bulbs like grape hyacinth or 'Hawera' daffodils, add a string of twinkly lights, and smile.

Give a different kind of plant as a gift this holiday season: think moth orchids, kalanchoe, aloe, ornamental peppers, and maybe a pink poinsettia instead of the traditional red. To extend the life of fresh cut greens and wreaths, spray with an antidessicant (like Wiltpruf) or keep a mister full of water handy—and, for safety and freshness, keep the greens away from fireplaces and other heat sources.

~~~~~~~ Growing Notes ~~~~~~~

Lawns. Sure, it's fine to 'mow what grows,' fertilize it once a year maybe, and never water at all. But most folks like a lawn—one kind of turf, no more than a few weeds, a neat bit of beautiful green to complete the landscape. Without becoming obsessed, you can have it if you can provide eight hours of sun, an inch of water a week, fertilizer twice or three times a year, and regular mowing.

Garlic. Plant garlic now for harvest next year, and be sure to peel the bulbs before planting them, to make them sprout faster.

Herbs and veggies. Though both herbs and veggies can grow alongside garden flowers and even shrubs, I make top-notch planting space for edibles so I can give them special attention. Practically speaking, putting herbs and vegetables in a raised bed or large containers means better control over water, fertilizer, and pesticide exposure.

Tiny seeds. Mix a bit of dry sand with fine seed like poppies, to help you spread the seeds more evenly. You'll have to thin less if the seedlings aren't overcrowded. Put the mix of sand and seed in an old salt shaker to make sowing even easier.

Composting. Compost happens naturally when organic materials decompose into a nearly homogenous material, when the original components meld into each other, their shapes and colors blurring into a rich brown, crumbly natural fertilizer. It is one stage along the spectrum of healthy rot: intact leaves fall apart and turn dark in the presence of microorganisms and worms; shortly the mass becomes leaf mold, a large particled organic matter. With time, moisture, and aeration, it becomes compost; left longer, the material decomposes at last into humus.

To make compost in one to three months, depending on the time of year and your diligence:

1) make a three-foot by three-foot pile with a mix of one part green matter (lawn grass, soft clippings, faded annual flower and vegetable plants, weeds) to three parts brown matter (usually leaves and small twigs) and chop everything to 2" pieces.

2) mix ingredients well with one cup of cottonseed meal or other organic nitrogen source.

3) use a fork or shovel to turn the pile once a week to aerate it.

4) water lightly if ingredients dry out.

5) bury coffee grounds, eggshells, and kitchen trimmings if added.

6) expect temperatures of over 100 F. in the pile within a couple of weeks—if it doesn't heat up, it's not working.

Rebuild to proper proportions, moisten (or cover to dry out in very rainy weather) and turn more often. Leave materials out of the compost pile that rot very slowly such as pinestraw, branches more than 1/4 inch in diameter, anything thorny, and difficult weeds like nutgrass sedges. Do not include any bones, oils, meat, or cheese from the kitchen because they are likely to attract varmints.

Easiest Perennials to Grow

1. blackeyed susans (Rudbeckia, especially hirta and 'Goldsturm')

2. yellow flag Iris (Iris pseudocorous)

3. red hot poker plant (Kniphofia uvaria)

4. lily turf and mondo grass (Liriope muscari and Ophiopogon japonicus)

5. daylily 'Stella d'Oro' (Hemerocallis)

6. Sedum 'Autumn Joy'

7. chrysanthemum 'Clara Curtis'

8. maiden grass (Miscanthus sinesis 'Gracillimus')

9. lantana (L. camara)

10. canna lily (Canna hyb.)

Dividing spring perennials. Early fall's the time to dig and divide the crowded crowns and clumps of spring flowering perennials like phlox, daylily, and iris (except the Louisiana type). Each crown must have a bit of green, part of the center crown, and at least a few roots to be viable. Dig and replant immediately whenever possible. Pot up divisions too small to plant out in the flowerbed in a one to one mix of potting soil and ground bark. Grow them outdoors over the

16

winter except during the coldest weather. You can put them in the garage or utility room to prevent pots from freezing.

> **Unbeatable Narcissi and Daffodils**
> 'Ice Follies'
> 'Carlton'
> 'Unsurpassable'
> 'Mt. Hood'
> 'Tete a Tete'
> 'Hawera'
> 'Jonquilla'
> 'Fortune'
> 'Geranium'
> 'Paper White'

Plant a salad garden. Fill a wide, shallow planter with fresh potting soil and compost, then plant a salad garden to grow right outside the back door with lettuce, parsley, and chives. Use two of each for salad and fresh flavors: red and green leaf lettuce, plain and curly parsley, onion and garlic chives. These plants grow best in cool weather; as spring heats up, they will bloom and go to seed. That means bitter lettuce, harsh parsley, and chives flinging seeds all over your garden.

Transition for container plants. Prepare houseplants for the return to indoor life by moving them into the shade a week or so before evening temperatures are expected to dip into the forty-degree range. By getting houseplants in place inside before turning on the furnace, their reacclimation to less light and humidity will be easier. Less wilting and leaf drop will occur with a gradual transition.

Bulb planting. Garden center shelves, catalogs, and your best friend all have Dutch bulbs they want you to plant this fall. Shop soon, but stagger the planting of popular spring flowering bulbs to suit their needs. Plant daffodils, grape hyacinth (*Muscari* species), Dutch iris, anemones, and ranunculus from late October through mid-December. But chill all tulips and true hyacinths for at least five or six weeks before planting. Put them into the refrigerator crisper drawer, not the freezer! Plant between Thanksgiving and New Year's Day.

> For better nutrition, use bulb fertilizer instead of bone meal whenever you plant bulbs.

Sanitation. Perhaps the single most important fall garden task is cleanup. Remove old flowerheads, trim perennials once they're dormant, and mow weedy areas around the garden. Not only will these tasks make the place look neater, but they also get rid of many sources of infection and infestation. Take a look at your mulches, too. Work rotting leaves, etc., into the soil below, and remove badly matted pinestraw entirely. Then put on a fresh blanket of either kind of mulch for the winter. Don't pile the mulch on too heavily: make sure air and water can still get into each plant.

17

Dormant and ultra-refined oils. As the name implies, dormant oil is intended for use during a plant's dormant season, particularly roses and woody vines, trees and shrubs. It is very effective at smothering insects and their eggs trying to find a safe spot to spend the winter in your garden. Even so, its uses are limited by daytime temperatures. Newer products, called ultra-refined oils, have a wider temperature range for safe use and are easier to mix and spray.

~~~~~~~ Smart Gardening ~~~~~~~

Dirt first: grow better roots, get better plants!

As rare as perfect pitch, naturally great soil can only be considered a gift. The rest of us have to work at it. Even those who are blessed with naturally perfect soil will find that cultivation over time changes its texture and quality. If you know about the Dust Bowl era, you understand the principle. Use the soil without replenishing it long enough and it turns to dust. Roots can't grow, so plants can't either. Luckily, there's one category of soil amendment that benefits every soil type—organic matters, or "oms" as I fondly call them. Just as that classic meditation mantra soothes the soul, organic matters ameliorate a variety of soil conditions.

OMS Oms are naturally occurring byproducts of plant and animal growth: manures, stable shavings, hen coop straw, compost, peat moss, hardwood barks, sawdust, plant processing residues like gin moat, which comes from ginning cotton, pinestraw, cedar and cypress mulches, and my personal favorite, leaves.

All oms have uses in the garden, either as soil amenders or mulches, depending on their size and shape and the rate and degree of their decomposition. Reserve bulky and long-fibered materials (pinestraw, shredded cypress, bark nuggets, and cotton gin moat—the residue of leaves and stems left from the cotton harvest) for mulching to take advantage of their longevity in the garden. Plan to dig or till in the smaller-particled, more rounded materials (leaf mold, compost, peat moss, ground bark, and composted manures); they bind readily with sand or clay and rot at a steady and relatively rapid rate. When mulching, building or maintaining a garden bed, or just planting one new shrub, be sure the organic matter you use is well aged—you should always compost fresh organic matters before adding them to garden soil.

Whether your native soil is clay or sand, it needs to drain properly, make nutrients available to plants, and create soil structure that encourages active root growth to sustain plants. The southern gardener's goal is to create a soil that drains better than the average clay or gumbo soil, yet holds enough moisture to sustain plant roots in dry times, even in sandy ones. The goal is a crumbly, friable soil that can be dug within a few days of even our wettest spells. To get a graphic look at the situation in your own garden, dig a hole eight to twelve inches deep and fill it with water. Clay soil holds the water for several hours, sand loses it within a few minutes—neither is ideal for growing a garden, but both have advantages to put into the mix. The glory of clay soil is tiny particles rich in nutrients and easily saturated with water. Sand's relatively big particles offer superb drainage with spaces big enough for roots to push right through. Somewhere in between lies that elusive 'perfect' soil; additions of organic matter effectively temper either one so healthy roots can sustain healthy plants.

Essentially, the same thing is going on in the garden bed and the compost heap. Natural substances decompose due to their digestion by a series of organisms. When you pile up leaves in an out-of- the way area, spread them on the perennial bed, or start a compost heap, those busy bacteria go to work first. They are always out there, waiting for organic material to break down. Their action improves the environment for the fungi and protozoans who follow them to lunch. In the pile or bed, you will likely find what looks like the white string that shoots out of a can when the fungi and actino-mycetes are active. (If you make a compost heap or pile up fresh bark chippings or manures to age, the temperature inside reaches well over 100 degrees at the height of this stage and so is called the 'heat'.) Next to move in are larger critters like mites and then insects and earthworms. Their continual presence keeps the decomposition going; you replenish the organic matter along with a dusting of cottonseed meal every so often to stimulate their appetites. All this good rot makes for a better rootzone—that means healthier plants, prettier flowers, tastier tomatoes, and ultimately a happier gardener, which after all is the point.

Enough of theory; here's what to do. Define the area with spray paint, string or by scraping off the existing weeds with a flat spade. Dig or till at least a shovel's depth into the native dirt. Six inches deep is wonderful, but four will do if that's all there is above the hard pan. Don't get into that. Once that's turned over, top it with four to five inches of assorted organic matters. I start with two inches of leaf mold (or even newly raked leaves in a pinch), plus an inch of compost (you do have a compost heap, don't you? If not, buy the best you can find) and an inch of chicken manure (though any aged manure will do). A half-inch of sharp sand helps in really thick clay or gumbo, but unless you're sure that sand isn't rounded river sand, leave it out. Finally, sprinkle on a layer of garden lime and a layer of granular fertilizer, each about as thick as sugar on cereal. The best way to blend all these elements together is to till or dig in a pattern: first work your way north to south, then make a few diagonal passes, and finish by going east to west. Last, rake the whole area level.

The resulting garden bed will be elevated several inches above ground level. Adding an edge of bricks, boards, or rubble at this point helps maintain the raised bed profile, but know that the soil will settle a bit, so don't overdo the edging. If possible, let the new mix rest for at least two weeks before planting.

~ ~ ~ ~ ~ ~ ~Vocabulary~ ~ ~ ~ ~ ~

Overwintering annuals. Known as spring annuals to folks up North, these flowers wimp out fast in southern springs but enjoy our mild winters if we start them in the fall. They include viola, pansy, candytuft, hollyhock, foxglove, stock, larkspur, calendula, and snapdragon. Lucky us, we can have their color in garden beds and containers from autumn through winter into spring, until they cook from increasing heat and humidity.

> Mix up only the amount of fertilizer or pesticide you will use at one time. These mixes do not age well. Mark and use one sprayer only for fertilizer and pesticide, and another only for weed control.

Minor bulbs. Usually defined as the less popular Dutch bulbs, this is a group of bulbs (usually small sized) so easy to grow and perennial that no one wants you to know about them. You may have to look in the bottom of the bulb rack for muscari, galanthus, lycoris, crocosmia, and the other obscure beauties. Many of us have watched our tulips topple in a warm spring, but this group won't disappoint.

Herbicides. In English, the suffix 'cide' generally means 'to kill.' Homicide is the killing of a person (*Homo sapiens*), etc. Products formulated to control weed plants are thus called herbicides. They work either before the seed sprouts (pre-emergents) or after the plant comes up (post-emergents). Their use is controversial for two reasons. First, good gardening practices reduce and prevent weed populations through mulching, regular cultivation, and well-placed plants that shade the ground below. Second, their indiscriminate use introduces chemical pollutants into water sources. Yet herbicides can be used appropriately and sparingly to hold back the march of especially aggressive weeds in lawns and flowerbeds with minimal environmental impact.

Tilth. When you grab a handful of garden soil and it crumbles through your fingers, that's good tilth, or soil quality. If soil is sticky and wet or turns to powder in your hand, its tilth is in trouble. Wait for wet soil to dry out before disturbing it to plant or amend it, and water dusty soils before working with them to preserve tilth.

Hardwood cuttings. As the growing season slows in fall, plant tissues harden in anticipation of winter. Small branches and twigs snap when you try to bend them because they are mature: they are hard wood. Many shrubs root well from hardwood cuttings, including aucuba, barberry, ligustrum, and Indian hawthorne.

Thrifty growth. When a plant is growing along fine, its color is good, the roots hold it stable in the soil, and as each new leaf opens, it takes its place along the stem with proper spacing. The plant looks right at every stage, and its growth is steady and attractive. A plant growing in a site it can tolerate, with water and fertilizer applied in adequate amounts, will display thrifty growth and the gardener can take credit for it.

.... FALL QUESTIONS

Q1. *Cutting St. Augustine grass.* How much of my St. Augustine grass can I cut off at once? I haven't been able to mow and now it's more than ankle deep, but I'd like to get it down before winter.

A1. St. Augustine should be grown three inches tall, but it sounds like yours more than twice exceeds that ideal. Whatever the depth of a turfgrass, don't cut off more than half its surface area at one time. Set the mower at curb height or use a string trimmer to carefully trim off two inches now. Then come back next week and mow closer to normal. With this approach, rebound next year should be no problem.

Q2. *Moving cypress trees.* I have a bass pond with an island in it that has a lot of cypress trees on it. Can I move some of those to the shoreline this fall?

A2. Absolutely. These wonderful native trees can grow near or in water, as well as on dry ground. Survey the ground on your island and transplant the trees to a similarly wet or dry area on the shore to make transplant less shocking to the cypress (*Taxodium distichum*) trees. Be sure to space them far enough apart. Bald cypress will grow rapidly to about 20 feet tall and 10 feet wide, then slow down but continue to grow, often to twice that size eventually.

Q3. *Tulip poplars.* How hardy are tulip poplars? I planted three of them last spring and one of them has never looked right. The others haven't exactly taken off, but had leaves most of the summer. Can I save this tree?

A3. These native trees (*Liriodendron tulipifera*) are quite hardy, but can suffer transplant shock like anything else. They need a well-drained site

and loose soil to support a relatively limited root system. I'd suggest using a root stimulator fertilizer this fall and again in the spring to see if they'll take off. As a side note, tulip poplars are huge trees when full grown. If you must dig them up and replant, be sure to space them at least 15 feet apart.

Q4. *Prickly Pineapple.* My child rooted a pineapple top this summer and now we have a huge, sort of spiny plant. What do I do with it this winter, and will it ever make a pineapple?

A4. Simply treat that treasure like a houseplant that loves sun—keep it in a warm room, water when the soil feels dry to the top knuckle of your index finger, and fertilize with a soluble formula once a month in winter. And yes, it will send up a flower spike, just like its relatives in the *Bromeliad* group, and when that bloom matures, you'll have a pineapple. Once that happens, it's a matter of time until it ripens. A teacher friend of mine needed faster ripening. He let it grow to about the size of a small melon, then cut the fruit off and put it in a plastic bag with a cut apple to ripen. Either way, it'll be the sweetest fruit that dear child ever ate!

Q5. *Rooting angel trumpets.* My angel trumpets have gone through a frost and are still trying to bloom. Will they come back next year? And I'd like to root some for my sister—can I do that now?

A5. Angel trumpets (*Brugmansia versicolor* 'Charles Grimaldi' is my favorite) are evergreen or nearly so in coastal areas and warm microclimates such as sunny courtyards. Farther north, they'll die down after a hard freeze, but most come back from their roots reliably. In areas where they keep their leaves, you should wait until early spring to cut them back, but if the leaves are off and the stems are not frozen, take some cuttings this fall. Root six-inch cuttings in water, then pot them up like houseplants for the winter, and set out in your sister's garden next spring.

NELLIE'S GRILLED EGGPLANT

Over medium hot coals, lay whole small eggplants right on the grill. Turn them (actually roll them) over as the skin sears all around. Once the whole eggplant is soft, but not so soft that it falls apart when you touch it with the tongs, it is done. Split it open and serve it as a side dish, or spread it on pita bread or crackers.

Q6. *Problem pansies.* I planted three barrels of pansies as soon as they came in at the garden center. One whole barrel died and the others aren't growing. I'm thinking they're getting too much water off my roof and might replant with Johnny jump-ups. Would those do any better?

A6. If too much water is the problem, I'd move the barrels! Dig around in that barrel to be sure your soil isn't infested with some root-chewing larva, and also to see just how wet it is about ten inches down. If that soil's very wet at that depth, dump it into a wheelbarrow and mix it with some leaves from your pile or some finely ground bark so it will drain better, wherever you use it. And be sure there are drainage holes in those pots. The old "layer of gravel in the bottom" idea doesn't work. If you can't drill holes in a container of any sort, grow the plant in another, slightly smaller pot with drainage holes and slip it inside the decorative one. You must still check to be sure that water isn't filling the outer one.

Q7. *Moving day landscaping.* We're trying to sell our house and the realtor suggested we put in some 'instant color' plants, like mums. Do you have a better idea, since the last time we planted mums they only lasted a couple of weeks before the flowers dried up. It may take longer than that to sell the house!

A7. For instant, impressive amounts of colorful fall flowers, my choices are garden mums and bedding asters. Both can be purchased already in bud or even bloom (if you're having an open house the next weekend). Your shortened season may have been the result of inconsistent watering. It's often hotter than we think on autumn days and new transplants can wilt and become stunted. Go with the mums and invest in a soaker hose to wind through them. Then use it. You can also brighten containers and plantings with variegated ivy and petunias. If the weather has already turned cooler, add pansies and violas. If it's still hot, you'll get another blast of color from impatiens and coleus.

Q8. *Sweet potato vines.* I saw those sweet potato vines called 'Blackie' at my sister's house on the Coast and took some cuttings. The vines have really taken over one bed, but I suspect they'll freeze, won't they? Can I save the potatoes?

A8. Just as sweet potato farmers dig and cure their potatoes to eat, you can dig and save yours for regrowing next year, whether it's 'Blackie' or his cousin, the screaming chartreuse 'Marguerite'. And you'll need to, since they're not reliable returners. Be careful not to cut into the tubers—dig carefully, then shake them apart with your hands. Put them in a dry location out of direct sun for a few days, then store them in mesh bags. When curing and storing, be sure the potatoes don't touch each other. Cure them on an old window screen for good air circulation and store in dry sawdust or straw. If that sounds like too much trouble, you can root some cuttings and grow them indoors until spring.

Q9. *Rearranging irises.* Can I dig up and move flag iris (*Iris pseudacorus*) right now? The clump has gotten way too big for the bed. Also, I hate the way the leaves look after they freeze and fall over. Can I cut them down before then, or must I wait?

A9. I know what you mean about these plants—the first clump of spearlike leaves yields great flowers and adds height, but then the plants spread faster than butter on a hot roll. Yes, you can dig and move them now, and believe me, if you don't dig and divide them every third year, the rhizomes will get as big around as your forearm. Go ahead and trim the leaves into a six-inch fan on the clumps you're moving, but leave the others alone until they turn yellow and fall over. This unattractive period really helps the plants, but it gives gardeners another reason to grow flag iris in the back of a perennial planting, along a pond bank or ditch, or somewhere else where they can be appreciated without close scrutiny of their sloppy habits.

Q10. *Storing seeds.* I saved seed from coreopsis and rudbeckia and want to plant them this fall. Is that a good idea, or do I need to wait until spring? How do I store them in the meantime?

A10. You can plant both of these kinds of seeds now, either in a seedbed outdoors or in flats in a cool greenhouse for transplant next spring. If you decide to store some as insurance against crop failure, put cleaned seed into a plain white envelope, then put the envelope in a canister with a tight top. Store in a cool, dry place, but not in the freezer.

Q11. *Fickle figs.* My brother in Louisiana gave me two 'Brown Turkey' figs last spring and I never got around to planting them. They're growing in big pots and look pretty good, but I didn't get any figs. Should I keep them in pots or plant them outside?

A11. Give those figs the room they need to grow—in the ground. Choose a sunny site on the south or west side of your house or another structure such as a garage. Dig a hole twice as wide and half again as deep as the pot, and amend the soil generously with ground bark, compost, leaf mold, or any other kind of organic matter to enrich it and improve its drainage. Keep the figs mulched and watered, and be patient. It can take as long as three years to get a good crop.

Q12. *Starting strawberries.* I want to grow strawberries, but it was late last spring by the time the ones I ordered came in. They never made any growth and died in August. Do you have a better way to start them?

A12. Yes, buy locally—ask for strawberry plants at garden centers or farm coops in late fall in the warmer areas and very early spring farther north. Plant them on a raised bed in a diagonal pattern and mulch with straw so the runners stay above winter's wet soils. Fertilize them with any vegetable formula and don't forget to water if Mother Nature doesn't. If you order for mid-spring delivery, look for everbearing varieties and treat them very nicely over the summer. Then you'll have your own mother plants for late fall planting.

Q13. *Pinestraw mulch.* Do you have some advice for us about mulch? My mother always used pinestraw, but I've noticed that what we put out last year looks dark brown and kind of slick. Do I need to change mulches, or what?

A13. Pinestraw is plentiful and cheap, and therefore, a very popular mulch. Since it doesn't break down readily, it lasts well and doesn't wash out of the bed either. However, those qualities also make it tend to mat down

and slowly stick together. When that happens, it's time to rake the straw out and replace it. The leaves you rake and use to mulch don't last as long as straw, but when they decompose, they provide nutrients to the soil and work to improve its structure. Ground or shredded bark mulches tend to be somewhere in between: longer lasting than leaves, but faster to decompose than pinestraw.

Q14. *Decorative driveway.* I would like to line my driveway with ornamental grass. My dream would be pampas grass, but I don't have room for it. Is there another one with plumes I could grow in a space about five feet wide and twenty feet long?

A14. Take a look at *Cortaderia selloana* 'Pumila' or compact pampas grass, but know that you'll get the same basic feeling from maiden grass (*Miscanthus sinensis* 'Gracillimus'), but in a plant smaller and tidier than any form of pampas. Once established, the maidens will bloom reliably with simple annual maintenance. Traditionally, gardeners burned grasses each winter to rejuvenate them, but this is illegal in most municipalities. Cut each grass down to a three foot mound after the flowers finally fade in January. I use a long bladed, hand hedge shear turned upside down to make shaping a neat mound easier. A dose of slow-release lawn food in June is a good practice, too.

Q15. *Coffee break for plants.* Our office wants you to settle a dispute for us. We have a nice collection of plants that we grow in the reception area mostly. There's a guy in the office who pours his leftover coffee into the plants every day. Is he killing them?

A15. He must not be killing them, or you'd be reporting symptoms of some sort! Just to be safe, get him to pour it in a different plant each day to spread the caffeine around. A little bit of anything, even wine or beer, has some water and possible nutrients in it that a plant can use. The problem with using too much of these handy liquids occurs when the substances in them become concentrated in the plant's pot. Alkaloids in coffee can, theoretically, affect the soil, making it more alkaline. An abundance of sugar (in coffee, beer, soda, or wine) may even attract tiny black ants.

Q16. *Leafless plum trees.* When my old plum trees leafed out this year, I noticed that they had fewer leaves than before. During the year, I watched some of the limbs drop leaves early and I think they're dead. I've never pruned it. Should I?

A16. Yes, you should prune out the dead wood now. Make each cut in healthy wood —a few inches back from the damage is best whenever possible. With the leaves off, look at the form of the tree that's left. Then in late winter, prune the tree. First even it up: if more of the dead wood was on one side, balance it by removing branches from the thick side. Choose your cuts to create an open vase shape in the branches for more flowers and fruit on your plums.

Q17. *Taming of the trees.* We moved into my dad's house last winter and have followed your advice to watch the landscape for a year before doing anything to it. We've made lots of notes and almost all of them involve pruning. The biggest problem is a sweet olive tree that blocks the path between the house and the garage. The second biggest is a 'Lady Banks' rose growing behind the sweet olive, leaning all over it. What should we do?

A17. Don't disturb either plant until after it blooms: the sweet olive this winter and 'Lady Banks' in spring. Then I'd try to put a trellis behind the rose and tie her to it, cutting off as little of the leaf area as possible to deal with this vigorous specimen. If it's possible to make a new path and not bother the sweet olive, I'd do that since they are slow growing. If you prune it off the path, it'll be one-sided at best and you'll certainly lose some of those fragrant flowers.

Q18. *Ragged roses.* There's a climbing rose on my garage that still has some leaves and a couple of flowers on it, but mostly looks pretty ragged and it's too tall, I think. When and how can I cut it back?

A18. Go ahead and cut out any completely dead wood— those canes that never leafed out at all this year likely won't recover. Survey what's left with these cautions in mind: climbing roses should never be cut down completely like hybrid teas, nor sheared off like landscape roses. They're a different plant, producing strong new canes from their base each year as old ones cease to be productive. Those old canes can be pruned out now or in February, but wait until after the rose blooms to do any trimming back to control its height.

28

Q19. *Problematic persimmons.* I have been trying to grow
Oriental persimmons for a few years with no luck. I've tried putting them in the ground and leaving them in big pots, but no persimmons. What am I doing wrong?

A19. Japanese (or Oriental) persimmon (*Diospyros kaki*) is less cold
hardy than the native species, but still can be grown outdoors in all of the south except the most northern areas. Grow them in virtually any soil that has been worked up and amended just a bit to insure good drainage, but be sure to water during droughts, especially in the first three years. Fertilize with a balanced formula made for fruit trees, and prune only to shape the tree in early spring. Give it plenty of room—they can reach 20 feet tall and spread wide, creating a wonderful shade tree even without the fruit. Japanese persimmons do not need another tree nearby to pollinate them, but some people say the fruit tastes better if it is pollinated. I say plant two trees of 'Fuju' or 'Gosho' (aka 'Giant Fuju') and enjoy the fall bounty, pollinated or not.

Q20. *Cooking pears.* We moved to my
grandmother's house and there's a pear tree that never seems to ripen. The neighbor said it's 'cooking pear' but neither of us knows any more about it. Do you know this plant, and can you tell me why they never ripen?

A20. That cooking pear is likely an old variety, 'Kieffer', that most
fruit growers shun as too hard, too gritty, and not nearly as tasty as newer selections. But don't get out the axe—harvest all the pears in fall as soon as they meet the touch test. Use your thumb to press gently on the fruit just beside the stem. When it gives just slightly, they're ready. There's nothing more delicious than the pies, butters, and pearsauce they make.

Q21. *Containing camellias.* The old camellias next to my house
haven't bloomed yet this year, but they're loaded with buds. I think I overfertilized them last year—one's so tall you can reach out the second story and touch it. When can I prune them, and should I fertilize this year?

A21. Camellias are not fast growing plants, so I suspect it's been
several years since you pruned that huge one! But yes, excessive fertilization (especially with cottonseed meal or another strong nitrogen source) can

inspire them to send up leafy shoots more than a foot long. Wait until after the flowers finish this winter, then you can prune off as much as one-third of the height. If you decide to fertilize again (next year or any year) use a formula made for them and other acid-loving shrubs like azaleas, hollies, and gardenias.

Q22. *Cutting back lantana.* I have some lantana that still looks great and some that has been cold-damaged, I would guess. Why is that, and don't I need to cut them all down before winter?

A22. Winter hardiness of lantana is a huge subject, both for gardeners and professional growers. Some are nipped back at 38 degrees; others need a real frost or freeze to send them into dormancy. Wait to prune until the stems and leaves are browned (or frozen) and then cut down the lantana to within a few inches of its crown. If the plants never go dormant, cut them back whenever a branch looks scraggly or stops blooming, or when the plant gets too large for its space. I have the old lantana known as ham and eggs that grows six feet tall and almost as wide each season. Unfortunately, it crowds the driveway at that point, so I cut it back several times a year. And, at will, I prune my other favorites, too: 'New Gold', 'Irene', and 'Sonset'.

Q23. *Pruning figs.* I inherited my mom's fig tree that has always made hundreds of figs. I didn't prune it for the last two years and now it's about 14 feet tall. Will it kill it to prune it this year?

A23. No, and I'd encourage you to get that fig back into annual pruning, both to keep it productive and to avoid having to stand on the cab of a pickup truck to pick the fruit. Wait until the 'dead of winter' (late January/early February) and remove only about four feet of height. After this year, just prune enough to keep the fruit within reach of a stepladder and remove any criss-crossed branches within the canopy.

Q24. *Unhealthy hibiscus.* I grow hibiscus plants in pots outside, but now they're in my living room with my houseplants. I noticed there is brown mold on the trunk and want to know what to do. The leaves have a few spots, too. They look like raised bumps about the size of a pinhead.

A24. Yikes! Get the infected plants away from the rest of your collection—they've got scale insects that must be dealt with very aggressively before other plants are affected. Once you've got them in another room, paint each and every limb and leaf with rubbing alcohol, then physically remove all the scale you can. I use a rubber dishwashing glove or a knobby garden glove for this nasty process—just a gentle rub with their ribbed surface works well. If the problem persists, and it probably will, look for a systemic insecticide labeled for houseplants—the product will be in a small shaker can in the rack at the garden center with other houseplant cares and cures. Keep the hibiscus quarantined until you're sure you've dealt with the buggers. (If this sounds like a lot of work, you'll understand why so many people simply buy a new hibiscus or two each spring!)

Q25. *Trees for the yard.* Can you suggest a big tree for my front yard? I want it to be evergreen, dramatic, and have flowers if possible.

A25. I have two choices that may suit your needs. To meet all of your demands, consider *Magnolia* 'Little Gem'. Evergreen with creamy white flowers like Southern magnolia, 'Gem' is neater in habit with plenty of smaller flowers each June. Another possibility, the dawn redwood (*Metasequoia glyptostroboides*) loses its leaves, but puts new ones on most of the year, much like the live oak. The dawn's texture and cypress-like leaves offer drama and beautiful golden fall color.

Q26. *Wounded ginkgo.* We planted a ginkgo tree last winter and it was doing fine until an unfortunate swipe with a string trimmer about a month ago took off its top. Now it isn't growing at all, the leaves have shriveled, and I need you to tell me—will it recover?

A26. Probably not. Forgive the offender and plant a new tree, but this time give it some protection. Put a ring of mulch a foot wide around that little tree to keep the weeds down and eliminate the need for trimming so close to the trunk. That mulch will also cut down on the competition for water and nutrients which the tree faces from the grass and weeds growing under it.

31

Q27. *Lackluster lantana.* My lantanas have a gray fungus or something on them. The leaves look dry, have tiny dots all over them, and dark gray edges. Should I spray them with something, or cut them back, or both, or what?

A27. I don't think fungus is the primary problem with your lantana. Do these two tests: shake a branch—if tiny white triangular bugs fly off, you've got white flies. Next put a piece of white paper under a branch and tap it gently. If the spots of "dust" that fall off move, you've got spider mites.

Since the time is near that you'll be cutting them back anyway, go ahead and do that now. Destroy all the plant material you remove in order to prevent reinfection. Next year, keep a closer eye on the plants and spray at the first sign of trouble with horticultural oil or insecticidal soap.

Q28. *Seeding Bermuda grass.* We've been trying to seed bermuda grass in the yard all year. We've planted twice already but almost nothing has come up. Is there any hope for us?

A28. Yours may be a case for a soil test. If Bermuda won't sprout, and no weeds are growing there either, I'd speculate that 1) there's not enough sunlight to grow lawngrass 2) you have a serious compaction problem and/or 3) the soil's nutrition is out of whack. You need a soil test, so buy a kit or contact the cooperative extension service in your area for more information. I'd consider seeding perennial ryegrass this winter to control erosion and puddling.

Q29. *Yellow jacket swarm.* My son was digging in my leaf pile yesterday and found yellow jackets. They stung him once and now I can't get him to go out there. What can I do to get rid of them and put him back to work?

A29. Wait until dusk, when the weary wasps have returned to their nest in the ground, then blast it with a jet-spray wasp and hornet killer. Use enough spray to completely soak the nest, work quickly, and go back in the house immediately. Yellow jackets sting with little or no provocation and you've given them plenty if they survive the flight from the nest. The next day you can dig out the nest, but keep the spray handy just in case.

Q30. *Alien aphids.* I know I have aphids on my roses, but recently I saw a photograph labeled aphids that didn't look anything like mine. These had wings! Do they fly and what else can you tell me about these suckers?

A30. The world of the aphid would be considered x-rated except that they're small and don't talk about their antics. They pierce almost any plant tissue and suck it dry if left alone, then excrete sticky stuff called honeydew. Then sooty mold fungus grows in the 'dew and leaves turn black with it, or you feel like it's raining while standing under an infested tree. As if that wasn't enough, they multiply about every eight days, so the ones you control today aren't the end of the problem by any means.

Yes, some have wings; others spend their whole life on one plant. They're also different colors depending on what they eat. But, kinkiest of all, the females sometimes lay eggs, sometimes deliver live young, and can do so whether or not they mate with a male! Controlling aphids is a three- step process: at the first sight of their pinhead sized bodies on stems or growing points, blast the plants with a steady stream of water to knock them off. They're slow to return; but if they do, or if the problem is more serious or in an edible plant, use an insecticidal soap or mix your own by my recipe: six squirts of pure dishwashing liquid in a quart of water. Spray often in order to melt their bodies as they hatch. For even larger infestations on prized plants, I use a spray containing azadirachtin (neem) or pyrethrin. It is also very important to practice good sanitation in gardens where aphids are a problem. Remove decaying plant debris, spray shrubs with horticultural oil to clean them up, and get rid of ants in garden areas.

Q31. *Conditioning flowers.* Can you give me some ideas for keeping cut flowers for a week or so? I can't seem to keep them from wilting too fast.

A31. Some flowers just don't keep, but many will if you'll cut them early (or very late in the day after watering) with a single blade, then drop the stems immediately into a bucket of tepid water you've brought along to the garden. Once it's full of flowers, fill the bucket up to their necks and set in the shade for a few hours to condition them for the vase. Recut the stems as you arrange them, and make a floral preservative of 1 t sugar and 2 t bleach in 4 cups water. Add 1/4 cup of this mix to a 1 quart vase.

33

Q32. *Painted hydrangeas.* I've seen gold hydrangeas and wonder if you have to dry them before you paint them, and is that hard to do?

A32. It's quite easy either way  you do it. Hydrangeas will often dry quite well on the bush and you can just cut them, sear their stems, and paint. Cut flowers will dry easily—just sear the stems and let stand in a vase without water. The flower color will fade to tan and then brown. You can spray paint anytime after the drying begins; in fact, a popular treatment is to lightly spray only some of the bracts for a muted look.

Q33. *A bath for hydrangeas.* I heard you tell a story one time about cutting hydrangeas and putting them in the bathtub to arrange for a wedding. Is that what you have to do?

A33. That's almost the whole story. Cut hydrangeas with plenty of stem, then sear it shut with a flame to stop the latex flowing. Next plunge them headfirst into tepid or cool water for a couple of hours to hydrate. Remove any leaves that will be underwater in the vase.

Q34. *Easy bloomers.* We're working people, and can't garden every day. But we want to dress up the front entrance to our property—a long driveway winds through an allee of crape myrtles, but they're pretty far apart. What can we plant along there that will have lots of color for most of the year and not require tons of work to keep blooming?

A34. First take a look at the area. Take into consideration where it's sunny all day and where the shade will give some plants a break. Fill the sunny spots with daylilies, hibiscus, rose-of-Sharon, chaste tree, cannas, and iris. Put a few of the cannas and iris even into the shade to keep the design flowing. Even if they don't bloom, their texture will be pleasing. As the shade moves in, plant camellias, sasanquas, hydrangeas, St. John's wort, and maiden grass. With basic care—just water and fertilizer, plus mulch and annual pruning to keep them in shape—your allee will welcome everyone with flowers and interesting plants all year.

Chapter 2
Deep South Winter
January, February, March

~~~~~~~ *Winter in the Garden* ~~~~~~~

The northern tier of southern states ('Deep South' on the zone map on page 10) is different in winter from the rest of the region, for plants and people experience the four traditional seasons. In winter, perennials go dormant, shrubs rest, and fruit gets plenty of chilling hours. As you go farther south, winter's conditions can vary drastically from week to week. This requires varieties of plants, especially fruit, that can be productive without uninterrupted cold. A week of freezing temperatures (sometimes with ice and snow), can be followed by nights in the 40's with 60-degree days. It's a roller coaster for everything alive. Many days are fine enough to draw the gardener outdoors, though, and you may find the time and conditions right to clean tools and repaint the trellises. In 'Deepest South' (p. 10) it's rare that a week goes by without one good day for gardening. Make no mistake, winter can be cold, wet, and dreary even near and on the coasts, but, thankfully, not for long. It's time to float camellias and watch the birds devour nandina and possom haw berries. As long as that last cold snap in March doesn't zap the flowers off peaches and blueberries, it's considered a good winter across the South.

Trees and shrubs. Prune your roses in February, following southern gardening tradition. Pruning is necessary for hybrid tea roses, beneficial to vigorous shrub roses, and a huge no-no for spring-flowering climbers like 'Lady Banks'. Wait until after they bloom, then thin out the oldest canes and head back the top if it's over the trellis. Tie canes to a trellis or fence rather than weave them through. Long 'arms' on climbers will give you plenty of flowers.

Starting with witch hazel, quince, and forsythia, a parade of shrubs come into bloom during the Deep South winter. The farther south they are, the earlier they will bloom, but their order of flowering is the same. As they finish their flowery season, it's time to prune a little or a lot. First clip out any dead or twiggy growth, then reduce the shrub's height if necessary for your design, and shape it for a pleasing form.

Dependably Wonderful Roses

1. Fuschia Meidilland
2. Caldwell Pink
3. Buff Beauty
4. Butterfly Rose
5. Lady Banks Rose
6. Red Cascade
7. Clothilde Soupert
8. The Fairy
9. Natchitoches Noisette
10. LaMarque

35

This season, plant, plant, plant. At the garden centers this season, you'll find fruit trees, shade trees, and shrubs of all sorts. Dig holes wider than they are deep, in soil you beefed up last fall. Capture as much of the container's soil as possible; if some falls out of the pot, work it into the site. Loosen or unwind tightly bound roots so they can spread and get established, or slice them a little on the outside of the root ball.

> ### PARSLEY LOG
> *Wash either type of parsley.*
> *Dry well.*
> *Roll into a log shape in plastic wrap.*
> *Freeze the log.*
> *Cut off only what you need*
> *and keep the rest frozen.*

Herbs and vegetables. Keep parsley, dill, and cilantro neat and tasty by harvesting small amounts continuously. Fertilize these herbs everytime the weather is pleasant to help them take advantage of favorable growing conditions. Plant flat leaf parsley for flavor, and curly leaf parsley for looks.

Plant a 'teacher salad' in pots or garden beds at the school: lettuce, mesclun, radishes, and chard make a good combination. Let the kids tend it and serve before school's out. Or help kids plant potatoes in stacked tires in the corner of the playground. Plant early corn and bush beans soon after the last frost date in your area (somewhere between mid-March and mid-April). If you want to order seed, get it done early.

Push the season by planting tomatoes early, but be ready to cover them for protection when March turns nasty. Make a quick hot cap with a gallon plastic milk jug: cut off its bottom so you can drop it over the little plants, cap side up. Put the cap on in late afternoon to trap heat, but remove it daily for ventilation if it's too cool to take the cover off altogether.

> *Popular Vegetables*
> *For Late Winter/Early Spring*
> *(In Order of Planting)*
> *1) potatoes 2) English and snow peas*
> *3) leaf lettuces 4) nasturtium*
> *5) corn 6) bush and pole beans*
> *7) squash 8) cucumbers 9) tomato*
> *10) peppers 11) eggplant*

Annual flowers and vines. Fertilize overwintering annuals: pansies, larkspur, snaps, stock, foxglove, and violas. Surround each plant with a band of flower garden food after a good rain each month this season. Or water with a soluble formula if the winter is dry. Add to the plantings as early annuals arrive at the shops or your seedlings get to be six weeks old: Canterbury bells, petunias, hollyhocks, and candytuft.

Get started soon with seeds or plants of nasturtium and sweet peas—both have bush and vining varieties for beds and pots. And plant

hanging baskets full of fuchsia, geranium, and diascia to get the porch prettied up for spring.

Vines often do best planted directly where they will grow. Put up the trellis first, then get out there on a warm day and plant scarlet runner beans, firecracker vine, morning glory, and, if you dare, cypress vine.

Perennial flowers and vines. Dig up aggressive perennials like cashmere bouquet (*Clerodendrum bungei*) and obedient plant (*Physostegia virginiana*) now to take advantage of cold weather to prevent resprouting. Pot them up for future swaps. Leave the hole you dug open to the elements, and pour in a little table salt for good measure.

Native oxalis, or four-leaf clover, and sweet violets bloom now and can be transplanted right after flowering. Mass them in shady beds for long-lived beauty with spider lilies (*Lycoris radiata*) and daffodil bulbs and a trellis of chocolate vine (*Akebia quinata*).

Curb the urge to dig and divide until perennials are up and growing, but as soon as the noses show, move hostas, daylilies, and other summer bloomers. Wait until after phlox, iris, and the rest of the early girls finish flowering to dig and divide them.

Bulbs. It's not fatal, but unsightly—those squishy, frozen leaves on amaryllis and crinum lily clumps after a cold snap. Don gloves if you must, but gently tug the leaves off, don't cut them.

Cut daffodils regularly for the vase to encourage rebloom next year in those varieties that can. As daffodils finish blooming, fertilize their stands with a balanced perennial formula. Don't mow, cut back, or move them until you can't stand it anymore—try to wait until they're at least halfway died down before you disturb the bulbs.

Except on the warm coastal regions, caladiums will get off to a better start in pots than in beds. Plant their bulbs (tubers, actually) in deep flats or individual pots of peat-based soil and ground bark, saturate once, then put in warm shade until they sprout. Move into bright light, then fertilize every week until you can transplant them when the soil warms up.

Groundcovers and lawns. Had enough of the winter meadow out on your lawn? If you like the show of wildflowers like clover and blue-eyed grass, but don't want them to take over, mow their little heads off before they can set seed. If more than half the lawn is in bloom now, consider spraying once with a broadleaf weed control. When groundcovers start sprouting, it's time to fertilize. Use a balanced formula with a higher middle number (5-10-5 for example) for flowering types like ajuga or vinca or even numbers for evergreens like Asiatic jasmine.

For a neat, nearly weedfree groundcover bed on a slope that's impossible to weed regularly, use weed barrier cloth. Work the area up first, then cover with the woven cloth. Cut an X in the cloth, then fold its flaps under to make a square planting space, and transplant. Apply mulch over the surface of the cloth and up to the main stem of each plant. Begin fertilizing with a soluble formula in a hose-end sprayer.

Fruit. Plant blueberries as a backdrop to the vegetable garden or in sunny mixed shrub beds. But give muscadines and other grapes plenty of room—put up an arbor with a bench or swing below, plant a vine at the corners and begin tying up the vines that will yield a delicious harvest.

Replace organic mulches around strawberries if wet weather prevails. At the first sign of graying leaves, flowers, or fruit, pick off the affected parts and begin spraying with a fungicide or try 2 tablespoons of baking soda in 1 quart of water. Neither method will remove the fungus, but either will lessen its impact.

When transplanting bare-root fruit trees or vines, soak them overnight in warm water mixed with compost or root stimulator fertilizer. The roots will be softer and easier to spread in the planting spot. Shop locally for the best fruit varieties for your area.

Prune figs while the winter's got their sap down. There'll be less latex to deal with and new growth will be sturdier than if you wait to prune. The best plan is to prune a little each year, but most folks don't. You can take down one-third of that fig without damaging it if that will put the fruit within picking range.

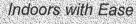

Indoors with Ease

Try these potted plants indoors. They like the same conditions most people do:

1) moth orchid (Phalaenopsis species) 2) Aloe vera

3) pencil cactus (Euphorbia tirucalli) 4) night blooming cereus (Cereus aethiops) 5) ponytail palm (Beaucarnea recurvata)

6) African violets (Saintpaulia ionantha) 7) kaffir lily (Clivia miniata) 8) amaryllis (Hippeastrum hybrids)

9) peace lily (Spathiphyllum 'Tasson') 10) Norfolk pine (Araucaria heterophylla)

Plants in pots. Get the foil off those holiday plants and toss it— quick! The foil covers trap water that's run through the pot, and keep pots of poinsettia and kalanchoe too wet. Give the plants a good soaking once a week at most, and keep the light bright until you can put them outside. If you overwintered Boston fern baskets in the garage or other marginal area, rejuvenate them now so they'll be porchworthy. Cut the plants way back, divide and repot if terribly crowded, and begin fertilizing with each watering to push new fronds.

~~~~~~ Growing Notes ~~~~~~

Seeding Indoors Under Lights. With a space no larger than the top of your refrigerator, a small fluorescent light fixture, a flat or two, some soil, and seeds, you can grow unusual, unavailable, and outrageously personal flowers and vegetables—and you should! Set up the light (get a grow light bulb or one that is labeled for both plants and fish) so the pots of soil are four to six inches below it to start. Use trays under the plastic cells or small pots so you can water from the bottom, and set them on a heating mat from a horticultural supplier (not a heating pad like you use for your sore back). Potting soil works fine. Sterile seed starting mix is probably better especially for tiny or dustlike seeds, but demands greater attention to watering to prevent drying out. Start seeds about six weeks before you want to transplant them, and once they sprout, keep the lights four to five inches away from their top leaves to encourage compact growth.

Row covers. Made of woven fibers that let water and light in but keep a variety of pests out, floating row covers may be the best kept secret in gardening. It's a simple principle: cover young plants like squash to exclude insects such as the vine borer moth that fly in to lay their eggs. In addition, when you grow greens under row covers, their leaves stay cleaner so there's less washing at harvest.

The catalog dilemma. The myth is that gardening catalogs begin arriving in January, gardeners sit by the fire and peruse them, then order for shipment to plant in March. Southern fires are often not nightly events and we're more inclined to be planting potatoes in February than waiting for them to arrive. Early corn goes in right after that, for the best chance to beat the inevitable arrival of the corn earworm. I am glad to have the flood of catalogs. Their information is often based on extensive experience plus the most recent data available for a particular plant's culture. If you can't buy locally and need your order shipped pronto, contact the seed company and beg directly.

39

Another myth about catalogs says that those from northern states are a waste of time. Most of my harvest does come from the southern standard sources, but I keep an eye out for short season flowers and vegetables in every catalog that I can find. The plant developed for a cool summer in Maine may perform very well in a southern winter.

Pruners and loppers. These are the essential tools for hand pruning. Pruners have a short shaft, curved or anvil shaped blades, and should always be found in a holster attached to the gardener's belt. Use them for deadheading annuals and perennials, shaping shrubs, and taking cuttings. If you use pruners to cut flowers for the vase, be sure to recut the stems with a single blade knife as you put them into the arrangement. Loppers are two-handed tools, with a curved or anvil-shaped blades at the end of handles between 18" and 36" long. A middle-sized lopper will easily cut branches up to 1/2 inch in diameter. If you have larger branches to cut, get a pruning saw. My favorite and most often used saw folds into its handle.

Bones Survey. A garden has to have bones—those permanent features that make it interesting even in winter and give coherence to the designs of other seasons. My idea of bones extends a bit farther afield than the usual paths, walls, and sculptures. Take a look at your garden in the deepest part of winter and sketch, take notes or photos to record what's there now.

In my garden, the hardscape stands out—fence, walkways, rubble borders, naked trellises, wooden chairs and bench—each stays right where it is, regardless of leafy embellishments later on. I also include evergreen plants in this category. If you've ever looked across a brown lawn to a row of cedars or Leyland cypress rising proudly with teardrop shapes, you know that shape is a permanent and very welcome feature of the garden's skeleton. I depend on the bed of Vinca major to be green and blooming along with camellias. Both provide a constant form to my garden design and take the attention away from the perennial border, which is a mess at best this time of year.

But in this southern garden, the bones also include tire swings, a rural mailbox, concrete ornaments, and a bottle tree. Each of these icons sort of disappears in the summer like bones under skin, but in winter, they define and reveal the garden.

Tree pruning. Best done in winter and while the tree is young, pruning daunts too many gardeners. Think of a puppy. Even if he'll be 85 pounds when grown, the control you exercise now in training him will remain in the future, and you'll be glad it does. The time to start pruning a tree is the

day it's planted. Prune out any crisscrossed branches and dead wood, and consider whether you need to cut off any low branches to encourage the canopy. Find a picture of a mature specimen of the variety you've chosen. Note how the branches stick out from the trunk, their angle, number, and distance apart along the trunk.

Read up a bit on the tree. Using Bradford pear as an example, you should be aware that without pruning to thin the multitude of branches that form the canopy, the trunk may be overwhelmed by the weight and split in a storm. Think of crape or wax myrtle: how many trunks make up this tree's best form? Those shoots that emerge from its base (sometimes called switches or rainsprouts) can be left on or rubbed off while small, depending on whether the form you desire is more shrubby or more treelike.

~~~~~~ Smart Gardening ~~~~~~

Plant sites: how to 'put it where you want it' and have it grow.
Every planting guide exhorts you to make a grand plan for the garden, where color flows through the year and textures mix like fine storylines in a novel. Labels explain this one's preference for sun, that one for semishade, and they all seem to demand excellent drainage. But truth is, gardeners see a plant they like and then look for a place to put it. The place is the thing.

Most gardens fall into one or more of four site categories, but most plants do best in only one of them. Gardens are sunny and dry, sunny and wet, shady and dry, or shady and wet. If you are aware of the conditions in each part of your garden, you'll always know where to put that plant you just had to have. And grouping plants together on the site they prefer makes caring for them at least an even bet, rather than a losing proposition, like trying to grow lawngrass in the shade or hydrangeas in afternoon sun.

Don't be fooled by plant labels, encyclopedia descriptions, or website tips unless you know the source and how it defines sun and shade. In our gardens, 'full sun' means blasting heat in late afternoon and is the province of relatively few plants, though the books are filled with it as a site recommendation. Mulch and regular irrigation help, but many plants simply lose water through their leaves (called transpiration) faster than you and their roots together can replace it in full sun. In my experience, seven or eight hours of 'full sun' is plenty to bloom anything, and to set tomatoes in abundance. I reserve the west side of the garden for heat and drought tolerant plants.

On the flip side, a plant's need for 'shade' is almost apologetic in many references, but a shady bed or two can be the gardener's salvation when temperatures soar. First understand that there are three kinds of shade: deep, high, and dappled. Deep shade gets no direct sun, only indirect and reflected light. In these conditions, every shade of green stands out and anything white, like a bench or sculpture, glows to welcome you into its comfort. High shade is that made by tall trees—here you can grow plenty of flowers and even sit to catch a breeze. Most plants labeled 'sun or shade' or 'part shade' will do well, but so will many plants that thrive in full sun in more northern latitudes. Their colors don't fade out, their season lasts longer with less stress, and your water bill will be lower. Dappled shade looks like it sounds, with sunlight dancing across the garden as sun and

Trees not planted often enough

1. catalpa (C. bignonioides)
2. althea or rose of Sharon (Hibiscus syriacus)
3. grancy grey beard (Chionanthus virginicus)
4. golden rain tree (Koelreuteria bipinnata)
5. parsley hawthorn (Crataegus marshallii)
6. star magnolia (M. stellata)
7. possum haw (Ilex decidua)
8. paw paw (Asimina triloba)
9. sweet olive (Osmanthus fragrans)
10. titi tree (Cyrilla racemiflora)

shadows move through low branches above. The areas of sun and shade move through the day and across the seasons as leaves fall and return. Plants designated 'part sun' or 'sun/part shade' are naturals for dappled areas. But watch to see how the sun plays in your garden along with the wet or dry conditions to expand your plant list—let the site guide your shovel.

Whether you consult a landscape architect or sketch out your plan on the back of an envelope, draw enough to know what the site is like (sun or shade, dry or wet) and what you want to do with it. Make a list: flowers by the mailbox, a tree that blooms and gives shade to a play area for the children (or grandchildren), a great lawn, tomatoes and kitchen herbs, a hedge of berries to cut for decorating, someplace to sit and relax. It's your garden, so you call the tune.

~~~~~Vocabulary~~~~~

Germination. The act without which no seed would even begin to grow, that is, the sprouting. Some seeds need light, some darkness, some have to be chilled, others must pass through the digestive system of a bird or mammal, and most but not all do best when planted in soil. The properly conditioned seed absorbs water, swells up, and spits out roots and shoots—that's germination.

Forcing. To make a plant bloom or fruit at a different time than it would by natural habit. Most gardeners have potted up narcissus bulbs to make them bloom for a holiday gift or put a poinsettia in the closet nightly to bring on the red bracts. Since both flower in January, in nature, you've

forced them to do otherwise. If the word offends you, say 'encouraging' or 'timing' instead. If they are in bud, you can force cut branches of forsythia, quince, pussy willow, or eleagnus into early bloom by putting them into a vase of warm water indoors.

Mini greenhouse. Any structure tight enough to hold heat and covered with a clear material to focus the sun's rays on the plants inside qualifies as a mini greenhouse, whether it's a mayonnaise jar turned upside down over a cutting in a four inch flowerpot or a clear plastic tent protecting early tomatoes. You can raise humidity around cuttings to encourage rooting and create microclimates wherever you want with minigreenhouses. Just don't forget to remove the cover daily for proper air exchange.

Bottom heat. If there is a secret to starting seeds, it's bottom heat to warm the root zone and speed the process along. Waterproof heating cables are designed to snake their way around the bottom of your flat or container. They come in lengths suited for any size operation. Greenhouse heating mats are self-contained; flats sit on top of the mat, so they must be the same size. Both cables and heating mats are thermostatically controlled. Use them if you are serious about seed starting.

Plant lighting. Traditional incandescent and fluorescent lights don't have the necessary red elements for optimal plant growth. Commercially available "grow" bulbs contain all parts of the desired spectrum, including red, and they fit a range of fixtures. But a combination of two ordinary fluorescent bulbs—one cool white, and one daylight—provide the complete spectrum needed for starting seeds and bringing houseplants into bloom.

Pergola. If you like trellises, but want to grow muscadines, wisteria, Carolina jessamine, and other truly vigorous woody vines and massive climbing roses like 'Mermaid' and 'Lamarque', you need a pergola. One is pictured on the previous page. If you have a wide, boring space looming in the backyard, you need a pergola. This classic (and classy) piece of garden architecture is a three dimensional trellis. Columns hold up an open frame roof; plants grow up, around, and over the pergola and people walk or sit under it.

.......Winter Questions

Q1. *Pots for a deck.* We just moved into a new house with a nice yard with a couple of trees and some nice grass. It'll be a few years before we can dig beds, so I'm thinking of putting lots of pots on the deck. What do you suggest? Can I grow flowers and vegetables there?

A1. If yours is the typical sunny south or west side deck with plenty of sun, the answer to your second question is absolutely yes. Three points to remember in planting a container garden anywhere: 1) big pots need to be watered less often than little pots 2) peat based potting soil is good, but better in those big pots if you add compost and bark to the mix and 3) by combining shrubs with perennials and annuals, the pots are never  completely empty, so there's always something to look at on the deck. Bringing plants up close to the house has other advantages: herbs handy to the kitchen, plus fragrant flowers, butterflies and hummingbirds near enough to your living areas to enjoy daily. Start shopping now for big pots to be the garden's focal points, and small pots to coordinate with them. Be sure to include a bench to sit on and enjoy the view.

Q2. *Wounded trees.* My house is old and so is the river birch tree out front. The tree has some rot in places where limbs were cut off before I moved here. Can I treat these wounds and heal the tree?

A2. Any old pruning cuts that develop soft rotten spots need to be recut immediately to stop the progress of the infection, and hopefully save the tree. Use a clean pruning saw to make fresh cuts in healthy wood, at least two inches behind the damage. Make the cuts on an angle so that water will run off of them.

Q3. *Pruning roses.*

When can I prune the roses at my mother's house? She's become an invalid and I need to take care of them for her. There seem to be all different kinds, even miniature ones, but they all of them have dead parts.

A3.

February is the traditional month to prune roses in the south. No matter what kind they are, cut out all the dead wood first. Then, for those that look like shrubs (including the miniatures), just shape them with light pruning to maintain a pleasing shape. If you have roses with three or four thick canes and very upright habit, they're probably hybrid teas: cut each healthy cane down to eighteen inches tall. Wait until after flowering to prune climbers, or even until fall, when you can take the canes off the trellis, remove the oldest ones completely, and tie up the new ones.

Q4. *Compost problems.*

Even though I turn it every month, my compost pile isn't heating or composting. I wonder if I shouldn't have put the pine straw in there, or if it's the peanut shells that are slowing it down?

A4.

Both materials are among the slowest to decompose, and I don't generally put either in the compost heap unless they've been chopped up first. Even then, a pile of leaves with pinestraw takes twice as long to compost as leaves alone. Start over: make several smaller piles that are two parts brown material like leaves to one part green matter like grass clippings, then add a bit of the straw and shells to each.

Q5. *Moving flowers.*

I must move some plants in the next few weeks and want your advice about it. Some are azaleas, camellias, daylilies, one rose, and a spirea. Can I dig and move them the same day?

A5.

Yes, if it must be done, a one-day uproot and move will be best. Prepare the soil in the new site first, just in case wet weather sets in. Transplant shock will be greatest for the camellia since its energy goes to opening flowers this time of year. Roses and spireas will be easy to move, and azaleas probably won't suffer either if you'll use root stimulator fertilizer at transplant. If you have a choice, pot up daylilies and other perennials and replant them in March.

Raspberry Vinaigrette

Put 1 tablespoon of prepared brown or Dijon mustard in a cruet or jar. Add 1 tablespoon lemon juice, 1 clove of garlic, minced, 1 tablespoon minced onion, half a cup of red wine vinegar, and 1 teaspoon each of rosemary and basil. Stir until the mustard has dissolved and is evenly dispersed. Add half a cup of raspberries, fresh or frozen, and 2 tablespoons of vegetable oil. Mix well and thin to taste with white wine.

Q6. *Corkscrew willow.* A flower arrangement someone sent me had corkscrew willow in it, so I rooted some in water. What can I do with the plants now? Will they grow outdoors, or should I keep them in a pot?

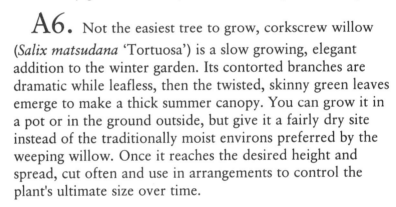

A6. Not the easiest tree to grow, corkscrew willow (*Salix matsudana* 'Tortuosa') is a slow growing, elegant addition to the winter garden. Its contorted branches are dramatic while leafless, then the twisted, skinny green leaves emerge to make a thick summer canopy. You can grow it in a pot or in the ground outside, but give it a fairly dry site instead of the traditionally moist environs preferred by the weeping willow. Once it reaches the desired height and spread, cut often and use in arrangements to control the plant's ultimate size over time.

Q7. *Moving groundcovers.* After growing a nice patch of ajuga and monkey grass for ten years, I need to dig it up and put in a deck. Can I do that now?

A7. Yes, but dig in soil amendments and work up the soil in the new area first to lessen transplant shock. Then use a sharp shovel to cut square foot sized sections of each type of plant, rather than individual plants. Dig deeply enough to keep the roots intact. The ajuga is shallow-rooted, but the monkey grass (ophiopogon or mondo grass) can be a little deeper. Replant and water immediately. That will speed the recovery of the transplants. Before winter ends, give the monkey grass a trim: cut off the old leaves, but don't go deep enough to harm the crown, which is the source of new growth for this and succeeding years.

Q8. *Satsuma orange.* My wife wants a satsuma orange tree to go with the grapefruit I gave her last year. She grows the grapefruit in a pot, but I'd like to plant the satsuma outside. Is that a good idea?

A8. It depends on where you live—satsuma is hardy from Zone 9 south, but can be grown in Zone 8 only if you are prepared to cover it when temperatures drop below 35 degrees. Pick the warmest spot in your yard—western or southern exposure, full sun, no wind—and go for it. There is no better fruit than satsuma and no better variety than 'Kimbro'.

Q9. *Pruning crape myrtles.* Is it time to prune crape myrtles? I see people doing it now, but I thought you said not to.

A9. My attitude about the 'lilac of the South' (*Lagerstroemia indica*, aka crape myrtle) goes against the grain of common practice. When there were only a few varieties widely available, folks planted them, then cut them back severely each winter to maintain their size. Nowadays, you can find crape myrtles in every height from ground cover to small, weeping specimens, to massive trees. If I were king, each one would be allowed to grow to its natural height, then only be pruned to encourage more flowers or shape the canopy. The reality is, yours may be too tall naturally to suit the space, so if that's the case, prune it now.

Q10. *New orchard.* I'm retiring this year and have decided to plant an orchard. I know I live in Zone 9 and shouldn't try to grow apples, but do you have any other fruit to suggest?

A10. Yes! For little or no spraying, try loquat, pineapple guava, avocado, satsuma, pawpaw, fig, blueberries, muscadines, Japanese persimmons, and oriental pears. If you are willing and able to conduct a spray program, there are plums, low-chill peaches, and even a few old apple varieties. Ask about establishing an orchard at your county agent's office. You'll get a list of tree varieties and lots of ideas. Seek out groups like the Southern Fruit Fellowship who have valuable experience to share.

Q11. *Luffa question.* A cousin of mine gave me luffa gourd seeds. Do you know when I should plant them? What else can you tell me about growing them?

A11. Wait until midspring to plant the luffa seeds and give them plenty of room, for they are vigorous vines. A long chainlink fence or even a big old tree makes a great trellis. Luffa is a squash whose fibers are used for sponges, and like pumpkins, needs full sun and lots of water to produce. When very small, soft, and immature, the fruits are called Chinese okra and are edible, though a bit too bland for my taste.

Let the fruits grow on to maturity to get the 'sponges.' Let luffas dry as long as possible on the vine, at least until the stems shrink back and when you shake the luffa, the seeds rattle. Both top and bottom of the luffa may turn a bit brown, and that's fine. Pick the gourd and soak it for two hours in warm water to soften the shell. Peel it to reveal the stringy sponge-like wonder inside, then soak it again in warm water for about one hour. Hang it up to dry. Shake the seeds out and save some from the best of the sponges. Now you can bathe with your new sponge.

Q12. *Baby pines.* Can I move some little pine trees that came up in my flowerbed now? They're about three feet tall.

A12. The only trick to moving pine trees is digging depth. Pines grow with one very dominant taproot. Think of trying to dig up a two foot long carrot without damaging it. Use a sharpshooter—a shovel with a narrow, long blade. Do remember that pine seedlings may be very different from their parent tree. Select the ones with the straightest trunks and most compact habit to transplant. They are easier to transplant when only a few inches tall. Do the transplanting during moist, cool weather whenever possible.

Q13. *Shrub roses.* Everybody says it's time to prune roses in winter. But my roses are bushes and they look fine. Do I have to prune them at all?

A13. No. The shrubby roses we know by so many names—bush, old, antique, garden, landscape, groundcover roses—don't need the severe pruning hybrid teas require. But in my experience, shrub roses benefit from a bit of pruning throughout the year. I remove dead wood anytime I see it, and shape the rest after each flower flush if growth isn't emerging evenly. If there's no need for that pruning, I snip off flowers as they age to encourage the rebloomers. I will leave some flowers intact after the fall bloom so the rosehips can feed winter bird visitors to my garden.

Q14. *Pentas, come back.* I really loved the pentas in my garden last year. They attracted lots of butterflies, but they look dead now. Will they come back?

A14. If you live on the Coast, they'll probably come back; otherwise, likely not. Pentas fall into that amorphous plant category called 'tropical perennials' and so are not reliably hardy where freezing temperatures are a common feature of winter. You can take cuttings in fall, or sink pots in the garden, then bring them into a sunroom or greenhouse in cold weather, or simply think of them as annuals and plan to buy more each year.

Q15. *Split pear tree.* My best Bradford pear tree has a problem. One trunk split last year and most of the tree looks good, but the split is really dark while the rest of the tree looks normal. Can I do anything to prolong its life?

A15. Your problem is all too common with this popular tree. Yes, you can prune out the damage, then prune to rebalance the tree's shape and its branch load around the trunk. To decide its ultimate fate, do two things: first, be sure that if it falls down today, it will not endanger people or structures. If it threatens to hit anything of value, remove the tree immediately. Second, take a picture of the whole tree showing the damage and put it on your refrigerator for reference through the season. If it loses leaves or branches continuously this year, or if the dark area obviously spreads, I'd say you're losing the tree.

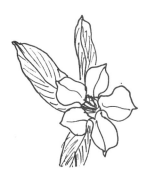

Q16. *Chilled patio plants.* Two of my patio plants don't look too good—I didn't do anything to them before it got cold and now I want to know if I should throw them away. One is a mandevilla vine and the other is a fern with big, light green leaves. Will they recover?

A16. Maybe and probably, in that order. If yours is a protected patio, the roots of mandevilla may survive to resprout, but remember that it is a tropical vine. I suspect the fern is southern shield (*Thelypteris kunthii*) that usually dies down, but comes back strong.

Q17. *Root crop failure.* I made a raised bed for my vegetables a few years back and everything does great except root crops. I've tried radishes, beets, and carrots, but don't get anything but tops even though the seeds come up fine. What should I do?

A17. Do you thin the seedlings? We softhearted types who love to grow from seed can find it hard to rip the little sprouts out. Crowded lettuce and greens grow anyway, but root crops must be thinned to have any chance of thickening and developing. Check the seed pack or catalog for appropriate spacing, then hold your nose and do it. If you're already ruthless with thinning, be sure the plants have enough water and fertilizer. Your soil may have a minor element deficiency, which also can retard root development. In that case, use a soil drench of minor or trace elements.

Herbed Pot Roast and Potatoes

Make a blend of herbs and spices: 2 T freshly ground mixed peppercorns, ¼ t salt, 2 T fresh, crushed rosemary leaves, 2 cloves minced garlic, 1 T chopped fresh parsley, ½ t chopped fresh thyme, ½ t mustard seed, ½ t celery seed. Set some aside and put the rest on a plate. Roll a 3-pound chuck, rump, or sirloin tip roast on the plate until well covered. Chop a large onion and put it in the bottom of a slowcooker (crockpot) and set the meat on top of the onion. Add half an inch of red wine, beef broth, or water (or a combination) to the pot. Slow cook on High for 3 to 4 hours, then turn to Low. During the last 2 hours, roll coarsely chopped potatoes (carrots, too) in the herb and spice blend and add them to the pot. Exact timing depends on your cooker.

Q18. *Muscadine grapes.* We bought an old house and there's an arbor that has muscadine vines all over it. When should I prune them and what else do I need to do to get grapes?

A18. Prune in January or February (at the latest). First, cut out the dead vines completely. Then cut the remaining ones back to fit the arbor. Tie the vines to the arbor, don't weave them through. Finally, look along the vines for the spurs, the branches that grow out at right angles and eventually bear fruit. Cut each one back to two or three inches long. Fertilize with any granular formula fruit tree food and keep the vines watered. Mulch with a thin layer of compost covered by leaves or pinestraw. Plan to fertilize again in May.

Q19. *Where are the iris flowers?* When my mother moved here

to live with us, she brought her iris collection. She can't give me any information about them except that they always bloomed. It's been two years now and not one flower! I planted the big roots in good soil, and fertilize each year, but what else should I do?

A19. By your description of the large rhizomes, I'd say you have

bearded iris. Those big roots need sunlight to set flowers. Dig the iris up, then rework the soil a bit, add a slow-release, granular flowering perennial fertilizer, and nestle them into it. Leave the top edge of the rhizome exposed, and, when adding mulch, be careful not to cover it up.

Q20. *Yellow leaves on hollies.* The hollies that I

planted last spring are turning yellow. It seems to be the leaves nearest the main stems. They turn yellow from the bottom up. Some shoots in the new growth are yellow, also. What can I do to stop this?

A20. It sounds like you have two problems. First the new growth

yellowing may be simply a spontaneous mutation; clip it out and the problem likely won't recur. But the yellowing of leaves near the stem may indicate a problem with the rootzone. It may be too wet, the hollies may be planted a bit too deep, or a fungus disease may have invaded the roots. If the bed has sunk, or if it's possible they were planted deeper in the ground than in their containers, now's a fine time to replant. If all else is well, drench with a fungicide monthly until spring, and use a root stimulating fertilizer formula to promote new root growth.

Q21. *More about holly.* I have holly bushes with lots of red

berries, but the bottom leaves are turning yellow and falling off. Is there something I can do now to green them up?

A21. Short of green spray paint, I don't know of a way to return

the color to those particular leaves. There are landscape spray paints out there, so if the in-laws are coming, go ahead. What's happening is the lower leaves are sacrificing themselves to sustain the holly (*Ilex*) because its nitrogen reserves are used up. Wait until the berries are finished, then prune the hollies just a bit and use a granular shrub fertilizer formula for acid-loving plants like holly, azalea, camellia, and gardenia.

Q22. *Rosemary.* Can I grow rosemary in my yard like a shrub? I saw it at a garden I visited last year and it was three feet tall with flowers! I love to cook with it, but thought it had to grow in a pot.

A22. Most parts of the South can grow rosemary as a shrub or even a small tree if you encourage it. The exceptions are wetlands and places cold enough to really grow daphnes and rhododendrons. I grow a rosemary about four feet wide and three feet tall in a sunny, shallow bed underneath a huge oak tree. It gets lots of sunshine but relatively little water. I too love to cook with rosemary, but remember to use only the newest tips until the bush is established. Pinch them continuously the first year or two to encourage branching at ground level, for many upright stems over time.

Dependably Interesting Shrubs
1. golden bamboo (Nandina domestica)
2. baby's breath spirea (Spiraea thunbergii)
3. Russian olive (Elaeagnus angustifolia) if you let it bloom
4. double flowering almond (Prunus triloba)
5. yellow rose of Texas (Kerria japonica)
6. glossy abelia (A. grandiflora 'Edward Goucher')
7. rabbiteye blueberry (Vaccinium ashei)
8. Camellia sasanqua
9. Oregon grape (Mahonia bealii)
10. weigela (W. florida)

Q23. *Dwarf azealeas.* How big will a 'President Clay' azalea get? I want red flowers but need a bush that will be about three feet tall to go under my window, and my mother recommended this one.

A23. I hate to disagree, but this Prez is a big daddy azalea once mature, eight by eight feet isn't unusual. If you like large single flowers,

look for 'Red Ruffles', but my first choice would be 'Christmas Cheer'. You can look them up, or visit a garden center this spring and easily find either one across the region.

Q24. *Winter tree planting.* I want to plant cypress trees and a green ash tree. Is it too late to do that now?

A24. No! Winter's the perfect time for planting all kinds of trees. By the way, if you're willing to take care of little trees, you should watch for the annual free tree programs provided by Soil Conservation and Urban Forestry offices everywhere. It's an excellent opportunity to add groups of trees to your landscape, and your labor to keep them going will be a legacy investment.

Q25. *Too much Bermuda.* There's Bermuda grass coming up all over the bed where I grow lantanas and roses. I fought it all last year, but I can already see it again. My lawn is centipede grass so that's not the problem. What can I do?

A25. I can sympathize—wiregrass as my grandfather called it is a common weed pest. Pull up the grass, then dig out its roots. When you are completely exhausted, do it again, then cut pieces of weed barrier cloth to fit around your plants. If you still have a problem, check the label on a selective bermuda grass control product. If it is safe to spray over your garden plants, you can consider it.

Q26. *Beneficial insects.* I got a catalog the other day advertising beneficial insects, but I'm not sure if they work. What do you think?

A26. I know there are fewer mosquitoes where there are lots of dragonflies, and that when I see ladybugs, damsel bugs, and assassin bugs on the roses, I don't see aphids. I also know that the most serious pests in our environment today are those imported from other parts of the world who have no natural predators in their new ecosystem. Think fire ants.

Before ordering bugs for release in your garden, identify your pest problem and select a specific control (the appropriate beneficial) to introduce into your environment. Follow the directions regarding timing

and conditions. It is easy to increase the natural beneficial insect population in your garden with basic healthy gardening principles: grow thrifty plants, identify pests early in their season, and use pesticides only with great care. Always select the most targeted control for the problem you have identified, and treat only the affected plants. This way, you reduce damage to the overall ecosystem, including the beneficial insects.

Q27. *Aerating and dethatching.* I'd like to know what you think about aerating and dethatching a lawn. Should I do either one, and when? My lawn is mostly zoysia, and very thick, but I have some other grasses in there. I want the zoysia, but have heard it needs to be aerated and maybe dethatched to grow really well?

A27. Aeration is the process of digging out small cores of soil to loosen the soil beneath the thatch in hopes of ending root compaction. Usually sand is poured into the holes. Thatch removal is more dramatic— sets of blades rip out the dead grass trapped between the grass and its roots to alleviate overcrowding that causes spongey lawns. There are aerators and thatch rakes to use by hand, but in my experience, their usefulness is more in maintaining the lawn than solving a big problem. These jobs are more often done by big, noisy machines and leave substantial debris. Both can be useful in the very specific situations described but neither, in my opinion, should be done routinely.

Q28. *Bean taste test.* Do pole beans taste better than bush beans? My grandmother says they do, but I don't have room for the bamboo tepees she grows hers on. I want to order some seeds. What do you think?

A28. It does take a trellis to grow pole beans, but you can go straight up with a string trellis rather than a tepee to save room. Some people do prefer their taste. But there are delicious bush beans to my taste, inclu- ding 'Provider', 'Contender', and 'Derby'.

Q29. *Cuttings in August.* When can I root gardenias and azaleas? There are some bushes at my aunt's house that I'd like to grow, but I can only visit there in July. What's the best way to do this?

A29. You're in luck since both can be rooted from their summer wood, provided you pick a branch of the gardenia that's not in bloom. The wood by this time isn't easily bent, but doesn't snap when you try, either—that's known as semihard or semimature wood. Take four to six inch cuttings, strip the leaves off halfway down, and stick the cuttings in a mixture of potting soil, compost, and sand. Keep the flats or pots outside in the shade and water carefully: you don't want the stem to rot before it can root, but a gentle mist several times daily will help keep the humidity up.

Q30. *Vines on a fence.* The neighbors finally put up a privacy fence so now I have a 30 foot long wood fence facing my driveway. There's only about six inches of bare dirt in front of it. Can I plant anything there?

A30. Sure, but I wouldn't suggest shrubs or trees. Get several trellises and set one up every eight feet or so. Wood, wrought iron, plain or fancy—the material doesn't matter so long as you like the looks. The trellises will become the notable view, so consider painting them your favorite color to set them apart from the fence. Put a birdbath and a few small ajuga plants between two of them, a birdfeeder on a pole between two others, you get the idea. Then look for tidy perennial vines to grow on at least two trellises to carry your design through the years—check out chocolate vine (*Akebia quinata*) and sweet autumn clematis (*Clematis maximowicziana*). Use annual vines like hyacinth bean, morning glory, and moonflower on other trellises for summer color and leave room for some bulbs in there, too. You could even grow trellised cucumbers! And that strip would make a great place to grow zinnias from seed.

Q31. *Feeding the soil.* I have heard you say to feed the soil and then feed the plants, but I'm not sure what the best substances are to put into the soil. I've always used a liquid fertilizer mixed in water, but it seems not all my plants thrive. So I'm building a new bed and want to do right. I'll be adding lots of leaves, but don't know which other organic matter to use. How do you know if chicken house straw is better than horse barn shavings?

A31. Either one works just fine, so long as it's been piled up someplace for six months or so. The decomposition process should be well along the way before garden use for either source. Bagged manures have been composted and sometimes deodorized, so some folks prefer to use them. But the combination of manure and animal bedding makes an excellent soil amendment.

Q32. *Shady planter.* There is an old concrete planter attached to the porch on my 'new' old house. The planter cannot be moved but is in nearly full shade. Is there a plant that I can grow there that will just be green and hardy?

A32. I would try cast iron plant (*Aspidistra elatior*). Its arrow shaped dark green leaves grow upright, it is shade and drought tolerant. You can fertilize it to grow and fill the planter, then simply maintain it by removing old leaves occasionally. They grow straight up, so I'd consider also planting English ivy (either solid green or green with a white edge) along the planter's edge to spill over it and complete the design. Then nestle small pots of colorful annuals into the ivy for color. Be sure to cover the pots' edges completely so visitors will think they grew there and be amazed at your talents!

Chapter 3
Deep South Spring
April, May, June

~~~~~~~*Spring in the Garden* ~~~~~~~

Once the nighttime temperatures are warm enough for a sleeveless stroll or even a swim after sunset, it's truly spring, and daytime temperatures begin their annual march toward 90 degrees. The warmup can be gradual, usually if rains are plentiful into May. Or, over a series of hot nights and dry days, everything blooms and sprouts the year's new growth quickly, as if to press for survival. Humidity increases steadily through the season. Corn and tomatoes seem to grow inches every day. These are the days that deliver wonderful flowers to every sort of planting. Annual flowers are fresh, not dusty, even in the median of Main Street, and formal perennial borders can be dazzling.

Now is the time to garden most seriously, to put watering systems in place, to get the transplanting done, to fertilize nearly everything in the garden, to repot houseplants, and to stake tomatoes. It's also the last practical time to clean out or install a water garden, put in a new deck or garden path, dig a new border, and add a coat of water seal to the benches and swingset. Soon enough, it'll be too hot for any sane person to even consider such strenuous tasks as pleasant garden projects.

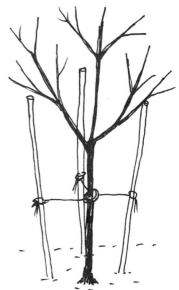

Trees and shrubs. The truth is, trees braced and bound with wire to support them at planting time never quite catch up with their free-grown counterparts. Take off those artificial supports as soon as the trees are rooted, during their first spring after planting.

Hugely overgrown, mature Formosa azaleas, nandinas, and climbing roses need a fresh start during the month after flowering.

If climbing roses are overgrown, first cut down their fattest old canes entirely, right down to the ground. Next cut the rest back by as much as half the height (or enough to get the rose back on its supports) so long as there are leaves remaining to get new growth started again. Fertilize, water, and as the plants grow, clip to shape during the season. It's easy to take healthy shrubs and trees for granted, but if you never do anything else to them, fertilize them in spring to sustain their beauty. Rake back their mulch and replace it: surround each plant with a half-inch layer of compost, one application of granular fertilizer (with insect control included if needed), and a new blanket of organic mulch such as pinestraw or ground bark.

Tip: Use newspaper covered by newly raked leaves for mulch between vegetable or cut flower rows. This combo will cut way down on weeds and rot in about two years. By then it's time to till and rework the entire bed using this ready source of organic matter.

Herbs and vegetables. To grow bushy, leafy basil, pinch it often. After each stem sprouts two new sets of leaves, pluck out the next set to emerge. That stimulates branching below and will produce new stems at the lower leaf axils, giving you bigger, sturdier plants with plenty of basil to eat.

Plant these herbs in the spring. Although the second two are perennial, the tender young plants taste best: borage (*Borago officinalis,* an annual which is easily grown from seed); basil (*Ocimum basilicum*); lemongrass (*Cymbopogon citrates*); pineapple sage (*Salvia elegans*), and salad burnet (*Poterium sanguisorba*).

Tomato suckers sprout from the 'V' where leaves emerge from the stem. Right in between, another shoot pops out. For more tomatoes, let the suckers go until they bloom at least once. To grow a few, huge 'maters, remove the suckers. You can leave them, cut them off and root them, or toss them in the compost. For even fewer, but bigger, fruit, remove a few flower clusters, too.

TERRIFIC TOMATOES

Nothing says summer like homegrown tomatoes. Buy plants locally, then give them fertile, well-drained soil (either in a bed or a big pot), six to eight hours of sun, and water as often as necessary to prevent afternoon wilting. Fertilize each week with a balanced soluble formula until first flowers form, then wait to feed again until first fruit are set. Mulch around the plants to prevent water stress and its unfortunate companion, blossom end rot. Pick tomatoes as soon as they have a pink tinge and ripen on the windowsill to foil birds and squirrels.

ROSEMARY BARBEQUE

Prune the rosemary, but save the woody stems. Strip off most of their leaves and immediately skewer shrimp, mushrooms, and cherry tomatoes (and anything else you like) onto the stems. Grill or roast until the shrimp is pink. The flavor is amazing, no matter what else you do to the ingredients.

Plant peanuts and sweet potato slips right before school's out. The kids can leave their garden space covered neatly for the summer, and these two plants will usually take the heat and neglect without missing a beat. This works well in the home garden if you're taking off for the summer, too. It's nice to have something to harvest upon return.

Annual flowers and vines. 'Recommended spacing' is just that, a suggestion, not a mandate. The design idea in a mass planting of any annual flower is to create a soothing body of color, not a jaunty series of colorful dots on brown mulch. Shadier beds need closer spacing to look finished; so do plants already in bloom. To encourage spreading in sun or shade, pinch plants and fertilize them about one month after transplant.

WATERING FLOWERS

The biggest difference between a good stand of flowers and a great one is most often water. Install an irrigation system, set up sprinklers and soaker hoses, or set your clock to get up early enough to water before work. But get the system in place and use it. Each time a plant wilts, it suffers, and flowers can be a casualty— few, pale, or short lived. Make smart choices in varieties, soil preparation, sunlight, and fertilizer, but don't count on Mother Nature to provide enough water for a beautiful flowerbed. Water deeply so it soaks in once a week whether it rains or not.

To grow zinnias and other annuals for the vase, think of their stems. They'll be sturdier and longer lasting if you thin the plants so air can circulate around each one. Keep leaves good and green by dusting lightly with sulfur or a flower and garden combination dust after rainy spells. Use mulch to prevent soilborne fungi from splashing up onto the stems. As you cut, leave four to six inches of stem to promote branching and reblooming.

Wait to plant heat loving annuals until the soil is very warm—moss roses, portulaca, hyacinth bean, and vinca will languish in cold soils. But they'll take right off when planted midseason and bloom all summer. Take the flowers off small transplants to encourage spreading and sturdy stems.

EASY ANNUALS FOR SHADY GARDENS
1) begonia 2) impatiens
3) torenia 4) coleus 5) viola
6) dianthus, especially Telstar
7) single-flowered petunia
8) perilla and 9) browallia

Perennial flowers and vines. There are three kinds of vines to know: clingers like English ivy and creeping fig will attach to anything; twiners which either wind readily like the jasmines or have tendrils like grapes; and roses and other sprawlers which must be tied to their supports. Jute strings work well for this task.

Five year old wisteria should bloom if you've fertilized and pruned it in midwinter, but if it doesn't, try this: cut the top back by half to shock the plant, tie up what's left to its support, or wind stems together if grown on one trunk. Then go a foot out from the base and cut downward along a dotted line in a circle all the way around the plant. That's called root pruning and it sometimes works to change growth dynamics and promote flowers the next year.

As spring perennials bloom, measure your satisfaction with their progress. Are they perfect this year, or better this year than last? Just fertilize and water this year, and slip out a few offsets to prevent crowding. Are there fewer flowers now than last year? Plan to dig, divide, and replant those perennials in late summer or early fall. Are they really crowded with no flowers? Go ahead and dig them now so divisions have a full summer to get established, along with the new additions you're just planting.

Bulbs. If grown well, caladiums can have bigger leaves and more of them: amend their bed with two inches of organic matter (compost or sawdust or an inch each of peat moss and leaves). Till the bed to six inches if possible. After planting, water once a week at least and use a soluble fertilizer with a balanced formula or fish emulsion. Keep flowers picked off immediately if they appear. Plant underappreciated bulbs for their flowers and conversation value: blackberry lilies, toad lilies, crinum, dahlias, hardy gladiolas (Jacob's ladder), Spanish bluebells, crocosmia—all these and more will add cottage charm to any garden with summer flowers. In general, plant bulbs no deeper than twice their height (that's four inches deep for a bulb two inches tall).

Daylilies and iris can develop orange streaks or spots on their leaves known as rust, a fungus disease that will weaken them if it invades the crown. Cut off damaged leaves, and then spray plants with fungicide or dust with sulfur. Plan to divide crowded plantings. Keep leaves dry by watering with soaker hoses when possible.

Groundcovers and lawns. Is the lawn plagued by fungus disease? Do not overfertilize in an attempt to regrow damaged areas, for excess nitrogen promotes fungus disease in turf. If the mower that cuts your lawn also cuts other peoples' grass, wash its blades and deck well after each use. A quick hosing between mowings lets any machine do its work more efficiently and can prevent fungus disease spreading from house to house.

Leave lawngrass to sunny areas, and fill the area inside the drip line of big trees with groundcovers and mulch. Good ol' monkey grass (especially low growing mondo grass) has hundreds of plants per clump, so separate plantlets into four inch squares and plant them on three inch centers in that shade. You can walk on it, mow it, or use a string trimmer to keep it neat, and plant daffodils there next fall.

Maintain established beds of dense groundcovers such as Asiatic jasmine with careful string trimming. Go over and around the bed with a light touch, just enough to snip the tips off and promote fresh new growth. Practice in a less prominent spot to get the technique down before taking on the front edge. Wear safety glasses, and don't worry if the trimmings fall into the bed. Think of the bits as fertilizer waiting to return to the soil.

Lawnmowing Tips

Mow your lawn at its proper height. Start at the lower height listed here, then raise the mower one notch at midsummer.

Tall Fescue. *Mow to 2-3 inches. Very popular north of Memphis, but sometimes it will grow in fairly shady areas as far south as Montgomery.*

Buffalo Grass. *Mow it as low as 1 inch to renew growth, or as high as 4 inches when growth is thick. Not shade tolerant, but it tolerates traffic when it is well established.*

Zoysia. *Mow 1-2 inches. Do not overwater to push growth, for though slower than most to establish, this one makes a dense, drought-tolerant lawn.*

Bermuda Grass. *Mow it down to 1/2 -1 1/2 inches. It grows in full sun only in warmer areas, and can be grown easily from seed in spring or fall.*

Centipede Grass. *Mow it 1-2 inches. This grass is touted as low maintenance because it grows slowly and so requires less mowing, grows best in warm areas with acid soil.*

St. Augustine Grass. *Keep it to 2-4 inches. This grass is fairly shade and salt tolerant, but the bad news is that it is prone to problems with fungus diseases across the region.*

Fruit. Now's the time to thin fruit (pears and plums especially) if small fruit or overburdened branches that snap off midseason have been a problem in past years. Shake the tree, or snip gently to remove about one third of the immature fruit. This action takes the stress off the tree and allows the remaining fruit to enlarge and mature with less competition.

There's no shade like a pecan tree, but making nuts in the home garden can be iffy. Fertilizer in spring can help. Use a fruit and nut formula with zinc. Once those cautious leaves emerge, it is time to spray if you seek to control phylloxera, a major pest of nut production responsible for knotted-looking, twisted leaves at the end of each branch.

Squirrels will pelt you with crabapples and birds will feast on blackberries, blueberries, dewberries, and strawberries unless you exclude them or run them off. Cats can do this just by hanging around the plants, but few are so inclined. Cover the plants with netting, hang fake owls and snakes out there, or put up distractions such as suspended pie plates, bells, and loud music. But know that the critters adjust quickly, so pick early in the day once fruit is mature, to cut your losses.

Plants in pots. Almost every plant you like can grow in a container, but match your gardening style to the pots you use. If you use a watering can or hose every day, grow in clay pots that evaporate excess water through their sides. But if you're less fervent about watering, choose plastic, because its water-holding capacity can be more forgiving.

Repeat the flower and foliage colors you've used in the garden beds to fill pots that will unify your design. Use the same plants again, or start a collection of easy-care, drought-tolerant alternatives. Add sharp sand to the potting mix to accommodate crown of thorns (to repeat salmon to red-orange), yucca (creamy white), bougainvillea (classic magenta or other bold shades), and allamanda (the best yellow anywhere).

If squirrels or cats won't stay out of your containers, discourage them with a thin layer of blood meal in the top of each pot. Reapply frequently until they find someplace else to dig. A water pistol works pretty well, too. Sit quietly on the patio and surprise them a few times.

~~~~~~~ *Smart Gardening* ~~~~~~~

The scoop on fertilizer. Even perfect soils stay busy sustaining the microorganisms and earthworms that keep the root zone healthy. Think of the drain on those resources: both desirable and weed plants compete with the critters for every molecule throughout the growing season. The gardener's task is to keep plants growing steadily. That's why I practice annual soil improvement, mulch nearly everything, and use additional fertilizers regularly.

It was told to me by an old farmer: once the pecan leafs out, there'll be no more freezes.

Twice a year, in spring and summer, mark your calendar to fertilize established trees, perennials, and shrubs with a balanced formula, slow-release, granular garden fertilizer. Look for a product that promises three months or more and figure it's good for about eight to ten weeks in most southern soils. Don't compensate by using more at first. Plan to give them a dose of soluble fertilizer about one month before time to reapply the slow release. To encourage new growth and flowering, fertilize more often and consider specialty formulas for specific plants in your collection. And if the plants still just 'sit there', get a soil test done and rework the soil. Spring and summer vegetables and annual flowers are gluttons for fertilizer. Feed them when you plant, and then weekly with solubles until flowering begins.

Follow with a sidedress (usually a granular balanced formula) for vegetables once the first crop is made to replenish nutrients for continued production. Fertilize annuals each time you remove their fading flowers, or weekly, with a flowering formula.

In addition to spring and summer feeding plans, I include some fall and much winter fertilizing. As soon as March seems to be warming up, the roses begin to take off and need nutrition to promote their flowering in April and May. At the same time, trees and shrubs planted the previous fall and spring can benefit from a root stimulator formula. Those new additions and any plants in stress get my attention in fall with a dose of 0-20-20 to promote healthy root growth. When planting annuals to overwinter, whether vegetables or flowers, it's important not to forget that they are actively growing, so use a soluble formula on them once a month.

Understand that the three major fertilizer elements are nitrogen, phosphorus, and potassium (N, P, and K, listed on the label in that order, such as 8-8-8). They are called macronutrients and are needed in large quantities. All the others you hear about (like copper, iron, manganese, zinc, and magnesium) are necessary in much smaller amounts and are thus called micronutrients, or minor or trace elements.

If a plot of native dirt will grow a group of common weeds, you know there are some nutrients in there. Most of the minor elements plus two of the majors, phosphorus and potassium, are likely to be present, but little nitrogen. Your job is to keep NPK and trace nutrient levels replenished, and your plants will thank you for it.

~~~~~~~Growing Notes~~~~~~~

Mulching. Blanket the soil around plants with organic material such as pine straw or bark to suppress weeds and moderate soil temperature and moisture. Mulch is also a design tool that makes the bed look neater and the planting more unified.

Pinching back. Remove the tender growing point on a plant's shoot by cutting with scissors or shears or by actually pinching with your fingertips. Many plants, including those with square stems (like basil, salvia, and mint) bush out nicely after pinching. Tall and floppy bloomers like 'Country Girl' chrysanthemum, New England asters, Joe Pye weed (*Eupatorium purpureum*), and boneset (*E. perfoliatum*) will have more flowers and less flop if pinched before July 1.

Insect control. Healthy plants can withstand occasional insect damage without succumbing, but when their populations build, plants can be threatened. The first step to their control is literally, a step. Walk the garden every day, both to enjoy its beauty and to monitor the pests so you can deal with them early on. When inevitable challenges arise, it's important to evaluate the situation with these points in mind:

1) be sure it's really a problem and that it's worth solving. Stinkbugs on tomatoes trying to mature late in the summer will take serious chemicals to control. I'd rather dump the plants. On the other hand, a spring thrip invasion in roses ruins everything for that season and will only get worse, so it must be dealt with.

2) choose the least toxic solution first and always treat only the affected plants. When it comes to bugs, I'll tolerate some damage in the name of ecodiversity, then stomp and squish or use a physical or naturally-derived control like oil spray, insecticidal soap, pyrethrin, neem, or rotenone.

IPM

Walk your garden every day for the pleasure of beauty and bug patrol. It's called Integrated Pest Management (IPM) and begins with observation followed by monitoring problems and applying a control if needed.

3) reserve contact control and systemic insecticides for intolerable problems like fireants and serious threats to prized plants.

4) continue to seek out alternative solutions—resistant varieties and biocontrols.

5) always, always read and follow label directions when using any pesticide (or oven cleaner for that matter).

Beneficial insects. Starting with ladybugs (actually ladybird beetles) and including the lovely lacewings (and their murderous larvae), there are lots of insects to encourage in the garden for their voracious appetites. The list also includes tiny wasps that don't sting, mites you like

ladybug   vs.   aphids

because they're cannibals, nice guy nematodes that lunch on grubs, ground beetles so ugly they're cute, and spined soldier bugs (same shield shape as stinkbug, but spiny and much better behaved), among others. Grow a variety of pollen and nectar plants, mix up the colors, and limit the use of pesticides to make them comfortable.

Biocontrol. When the natural beneficial insects aren't numerous enough, or you have a specific problem such as cabbage worms, turn to biocontrols. These products include sprays containing parasitic bacteria, lacewing larvae delivered ready to hatch, and spores to control Japanese beetle larvae.

But understand that there is a downside to wreaking havoc on all moth or butterfly (*Lepidoptera*) larvae. You may be killing nasty cabbage worms, but are also destroying delightful monarch butterflies, so never spray biocontrols wholesale across the garden. Please remember that biocontrols and pesticides derived from natural sources are still lethal substances, and use them according to label directions.

~~~~~~~ *Vocabulary* ~~~~~~~

Perennial crown. When you poke around in a perennial plant, there's always a center someplace under the leaves and stems. Sometimes this crown is dome-shaped and almost woody, with stems sticking out every which way. Other crowns lie flat in a rosette on the ground. They are the heart and soul of every plant that goes dormant after flowering and resumes growth after a rest period. The crown generates both new roots and new shoots every year, and its care is paramount to the plant's survival. Do not allow crowns to sit in water or they will rot.

Lawn greenup. The magic moment when you glance out the window to see the turfgrass has changed from brown to green. If you have a mow-what-grows lawn (a combination of grasses and broadleaf plants), it greens up as soon as the first ones sprout and you can fertilize it anytime in spring or summer. True turfs green up at different, fairly predictable times. St. Augustine comes first, then centipede, buffalograss, and zoysia. Bermudagrass is generally the last popular southern turf to green up.

Fertilizer. Products containing plant nutrients and applied either in water or as an addition to the soil. Their origin determines whether they are organic (derived from naturally occurring sources, such as seaweed or cottonseed meal) or inorganic (manufactured chemicals like nitrate of soda). Solubles dissolve easily in water and can be balanced (20-20-20) or specialized (5-33-10 for flowers). They work quickly but are relatively short-lived and so are applied often. Granular fertilizers generally last longer in the soil and the best offer both fast and slow release nitrogen sources to prolong its effect in addition to the longer-lasting phosphorus and potassium. They are released in one of two ways, depending on the product: through irrigation or soil temperature.

Softwood cuttings. Tender young sprouts from shrubs in spring which will not break or crush when you bend them over. The wood is 'soft' and can make excellent cuttings especially in plants whose later growth is twiggy such as abelia, bottlebrush, clematis, and several magnolias.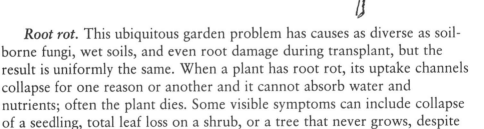

Root rot. This ubiquitous garden problem has causes as diverse as soil-borne fungi, wet soils, and even root damage during transplant, but the result is uniformly the same. When a plant has root rot, its uptake channels collapse for one reason or another and it cannot absorb water and nutrients; often the plant dies. Some visible symptoms can include collapse of a seedling, total leaf loss on a shrub, or a tree that never grows, despite good efforts at water and fertilizer.

.......SPRING QUESTIONS

Q1. *Weed control.* I've gotten conflicting information about what's best to control weeds in my lawn. Should I use a granular product or a spray? And what about rainy weather: should I treat the lawn before or after it rains?

A1. First off, understand my point of view. I don't mind a few non-turf plants in the lawn, but you're losing good grass when wild onions, dense clovers, or dollar weed have taken over half of the lawn or more. I know that if gardeners would take better care of the lawn in the first place, there'd be fewer weeds to control, and we could spend our money on more plants. Given decent soil and sunlight, regular fertilization, adequate water, and regular mowing at the height right for your grass, your lawn should thrive. Now, as to your questions: use a spray product to control existing weeds. Make sure it is labeled for your turf and weeds, then read and follow the label directions exactly as to amounts and preferred conditions, including rainy weather. Once you get them under control this year, prevent the problems by using a granular, pre-emergent weed control every fall and spring.

Q2. *Compost topdressing.* I want to put a compost topdressing on my lawn as you advised someone to do if they had dead spots. How much do I use and how do I prepare the area?

A2. First loosen the soil in the dead spots by raking it lightly. Sift your own or purchase finely screened compost and apply half an inch across the top of the entire lawn. Drag the back of a stiff garden rake lightly across the grass to send the compost into the thatch. Water afterward if the weather is dry that week.

Q3. *Protecting flowers from a cold snap.* When a late cold snap threatens my flowers, what should I cover them up with? I've used plastic and bed sheets, but still some things suffer. Which is better?

A3. In general, I prefer not to cover anything at all, having observed that established plants will survive even if they lose a few buds to cold nights. I do cut any flowers that are even half opened, and make sure perennial crowns or roots are mulched well. If you cover plants with plastic, be sure to remove it every morning to allow for proper air circulation around the plants and prevent damage caused when the sun focuses through the plastic. Cotton bed sheets offer less insulation and should also be removed if the day heats up.

FLOWERFUL SALAD

Though many flowers are edible, many people are shy to pop a pansy in their mouth. Shred a colorful combination of edible bloomers, top the salad greens with the mix, and smile when they ask you what it is. Grow your own edibles, or buy from an organic market so you know that they have not been sprayed with pesticides you shouldn't eat. Dianthus, pansy, and marigold top my list for flavor. As a grower friend of mine told me, the fact that it's edible doesn't mean it tastes good!

Q4. *Planting on a slope.* There's a slope behind my house that I want to plant something on to prevent erosion and have it look good all year. It's about six feet almost straight down to the neighbor's fence. What can you suggest?

A4. You're looking for a plant that 1) spreads wide and fast, so you don't have to plant dozens to get coverage 2) is evergreen or nearly so, and 3) can grow in the site's available water and sunlight. My choices include *Vinca major*, English or Algerian ivy (*Hedera* spp.), and the poorly named common winter creeper (*Euonymus*).

Q5. *Caring for cherry trees.* I planted two cherry trees—I think their name is 'Yoshima'—several years ago. One blooms divinely and the other never has. I drill holes and feed them 8-8-8 once each summer. Is there anything else I can do?

A5. Yes, two things come to mind. First, change the fertilizer formula and timing. Switch from 8-8-8 to a flowering tree fertilizer formula this season—ask for something to use on crape myrtles. Then use 0-20-20 in September to boost the nutrients that favor flowering. Second, prune the trees next January to shape them and remove any criss-crossed branches. This may stimulate flowering. If it doesn't, consider root pruning the shy bloomer. Make shovel cuts in a dotted line around the tree's trunk about twelve inches out from it in the fall.

Q6. *Troublesome tomatoes.* I planted tomatoes last week and they wilted right away and haven't recovered yet. What can I do?

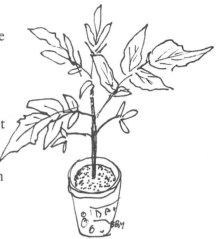

A6. Chalk their problems up to transplant shock. Pull them up and go buy some new plants and a bottle of root stimulator fertilizer. Be sure neither the tomato plants nor the soil is bone dry, and wait until late afternoon to transplant in sunny weather. Lightly squeeze the plastic cell holding the plant to loosen the roots, then gently slide it out and plant with one inch of stem (or more) buried with the rootball. Pull up the soil, water in with the fertilizer, and keep the plants well watered until they take off.

Q7. *Falling peaches.* The peach trees I planted a few years ago have grown just great, but most of the fruit falls off. What can I do to get the fruit to stay on the tree and ripen?

A7. Peach trees are particularly exuberant—they put on many more fruit than the tree can sustain to harvest. But they are not the easiest fruit to grow, requiring more pruning and pest control than figs or plums. This year, take off every other fruit that has formed, then water the tree well once a week until harvest. Next year, mark your calendar to prune the peach in winter. Thin out the interior branches so the tree looks like an empty vase. This lets sunshine in, and reduces the number of fruit, too.

Q8. *Saving trees from lightning.* Lightning hit the big tree right next to my house and one of the two big trunks was lost. Now I see limbs falling off every week. What can I do to save it?

A8. Not much, unfortunately. A tree so damaged is a hazard that will only get worse. If it is within falling range of your home (or your neighbor's) I'd have it removed professionally right away. If not deemed a hazard, prune the damage out and leave the tree trunk for wildlife habitat. You might even get a family of woodpeckers to set up housekeeping! Or use it as a trellis for a truly huge vine like cross vine (*Bignonia capreolata*).

Q9. *Trouble with tulips.* Why don't tulips come back like daffodils? When I lived in Ohio, both performed well for years.

A9. It's partly because of their nature and partly because of our climate. Unlike daffodils and most other bulbs, tulips form their entire flower inside the bulb before it ever sprouts. In fact, if you slice a viable tulip bulb in half, you can identify each flower part separately. Southern summers are almost all too hot to induce the new tulip flower to form. Many daffodil varieties, on the other hand, thrive during the summer here, multiply, and provide more flowers each year until they crowd themselves and must be divided like other perennials.

Q10. *Fungicide for roses.* Can you suggest a fungicide for my roses? I have three beds of all kinds and some get black spot very badly.

A10. Know three things: 1) roses that are susceptible to black spot will always get it to one extent or another; if you hate to spray, choose resistant varieties. 2) any fungicide (such as Neem or Funginex) labeled for roses with black spot works at that moment, but some roses must be sprayed weekly to control the problem. If you must spray that often, rotate the products for better effect. 3) cultural practices help reduce the problem: don't crowd the plants together, keep the ground around them clear of weeds and replace mulch annually, and spray the plants with a light oil spray and/or lime sulfur while dormant.

Q11. *Digging up holly seedlings.* The old holly bushes at my mother's house are real reliable berry producers and I'd like to have some. Sometimes there are seedlings in the bed. Can I dig those up?

A11. You can, and I might, just for curiosity. But most hollies require both male and female plants to be present for berries to form. Take a look at the bushes now and note which ones have the most berries and which do not, then plan to root cuttings of both in July or August. Many shrubs root easily at that time of the year, when the 'semihard' wood will still bend easily.

Q12. *To replant or not to replant.* Is it the right time to replant areas in my lawn? Which do your prefer, centipede or zoysia?

A12. Spring is an excellent time to replant dead lawn areas. Just work up the bad spots slightly by adding a bit of compost, then replant. I think each grass has its assets: centipede grows slowly, which can be frustrating, but the ultimate result is a lower maintenance lawn than the fast-growing zoysia. If foot traffic is high on your lawn, choose the thin-bladed, fine textured zoysia.

Q13. *Potatoes, please.* I want to grow potatoes, like I did back in Ohio, but I've heard that you grow them in mulch down here. How is that, and what variety would you suggest?

A13. Prepare the soil in the fall for planting in January or February (or late August for fall potatoes) by digging or tilling and adding compost, manure, and any other organic matter to the native soil. Cut potatoes into pieces and let them callus over (see A 14 below) for a day before planting. Nestle each piece into the soil 10 to 12 inches apart, but barely cover with soil. Cover them with mulch a foot deep. Hay works

very well for this, as does leaf mold. The idea is to give them an environment better than our dense soils to grow in. As the stems grow, pull up more mulch around them. Be sure to keep the tubers covered and out of sunlight so they don't turn green, as you may if you eat green-skinned potatoes. My favorite potato of all is Red LaSoda, developed at LSU and unsurpassed for taste in my book. Get it, or Irish (white) seed potatoes at your local coop or garden center, or order from a source that can get them to you before mid-February.

Q14. *Second helping of potatoes.* My mother grew potatoes every year, but I've never seen anyone cut them the way she did. Do you cut them into pieces or plant them whole? And how do you know when they're ready to harvest?

A14. When you harvest depends in part on how soon you're able to plant the potatoes. If January's a real soaker, February's ok for planting, but it all depends on soil conditions. Cut the potatoes for planting into chunks with at least two spots (called 'eyes', they're the growing points). Wait a day or so to plant so the potatoes can form a thick skin (called a callus) that speeds sprouting in the soil. When you plant in fall, potatoes should be left whole, to prevent diseases prevalent at that time of year. In May, start pulling the mulch back to harvest small, 'new' potatoes. Let the flowers finish and the stalks begin to die down before you begin to gently dig around in the top layer of soil and leaves to see if any potatoes are ready. If you can plant before Valentine's Day, you can join my family in a Mother's Day tradition: new potatoes and fresh green beans (bush beans planted in March.) Dig the rest within a month. If you leave them in the ground too long, they will rot. Use your gloved hand (or a trowel or hand cultivator if you're very careful) to gently remove the top layers of soil to reveal the potatoes. Go slowly!

- Floating row covers are useful all year to exclude insects. Woven fabric lets sun and water in, but camouflages the plants below.

- Tie tomatoes with soft cotton (old tee shirts are excellent) and tie roses and fruit vines with jute string. Never tie up plants with plastic or wire—either will cut right through the stems.

- The first thing a seed does on its way to sprouting is to soak up water, but some seeds don't take this step willingly. Soak seeds with hard coats like okra and morning glory. Put them in a jar of warm (not hot) water, swirl it around, and let it sit for a couple of hours before planting.

Q15. *Locating loquat.* When I lived in Pakistan, we grew a delicious fruit called loquat. Can I grow it here? The winters are somewhat colder, but the summers are not much different. Do you know this fruit and where I can get some?

A15. You and I share a love of loquat

with many other people. Yes, the plants are hardy in the Southeast, but some bear fruit better than others. Look for *Eriobotrya japonica* if you live in coastal areas (Zones 9 to 11), but get *E. deflexa* if you live farther north. Or you can grow either one in a large pot or espaliered on a warm brick wall. Even if it never fruits, loquat is a beautiful tree with dark green leaves and rough texture. The yellow orbs are sweet, yet tart, and I love them.

Q16. *Groundcover, not grass.* After

years of trying to grow grass under the trees in my backyard, I've listened to you and am ready to try groundcovers instead. Do I need to kill the weeds and grass that are in there? Can I add dirt under the trees?

A16. No, just mow or use

a string trimmer to cut the undesirables down very close to the ground, then turn over a shallow patch to plant in. Follow the planting with two inches of organic matter (perhaps the leaf mold made from last year's leaf fall) and remember to water a bit more this year. The competition with the tree can be tough, but if you start with small plants and encourage them with a fertilizer mixed in water, they should take off. Never add more than half an inch to an inch of soil under trees, or you'll risk root damage.

Great annual vines

Here are vines that can provide quick, full cover for beds, cascade from a big flowerpot, and grow on a string trellis over an old swingset frame to make some welcome shade.

1. morning glory (Ipomoea nil)

2. moonflower (I. alba)

3. sweet potato vine (Ipoemoea 'Blackie', I. 'Marguerite')

4. 'tater vine (Dioscorea bulbifera)

5. cypress vine or cardinal climber (Ipomoea quamoclit)

6. Chilean glory vine (Eccremocarpus scaber)

7. Spanish flag or mina lobata (Quamoclit lobata)

8. luffa (L. aegyptiaca), birdhouse and dipper gourds (Lagenaria siceraria)

9. scarlet runner bean (Phaseolus coccineus)

10. hyacinth bean (Dolichos lablab)

73

Q17. *Disappearing irises.* My iris bed started out with blue, purple, white, yellow, and cream colored flowers. I know that's what was there because I planted them all and they bloomed fine for the first few years. Now there are just as many flowers but they're all white. What happened?

A17. The case of the 'mysterious disappearing iris' causes consternation and everyone offers explanations. Here's mine. Irises do not change color, but a healthy stand of whites will dominate (after a few years) over fancier, less vigorous hybrids. Eventually, the whites spread through the bed, the others do not, and as the bed gets crowded, only the whites survive to bloom. The solution? Dig and divide the iris every other year to keep them under control. Or plant groups of iris within a bed and use daylilies or another vigorous perennial to separate them.

Q18. *The Fairy.* 'The Fairy' is one of my favorite roses, but I don't know when to prune it because it blooms all the time. This year I didn't prune at all, and now part of it is really tall and the rest is kind of stunted-looking. Can I prune now?

A18. Old garden roses like yours can be pruned almost any time. First, remove the dead and twiggy wood, then reshape the rose to balance the shape. Fertilize lightly and watch for new growth and blooms in about six weeks. Strip the lower leaves off six-inch pieces of healthy trimmings and root in a mix of compost and sand—nothing is easier to root.

Q19. *Mulching fig trees.* Should I mulch my fig tree? I pruned it back by half its height last winter and fed it cottonseed meal last week.

A19. Yes, by all means mulch under that fig. Extend a blanket about two inches deep of pine straw or leaf mold around the trunk and outward to cover the area wet by rainfall dripping from the canopy of your tree (the 'drip line'). Ideally, you'd have pruned that fig in January, but

there's still a chance you'll get figs to ripen as a late summer crop. Cottonseed meal works well, but if you find that you get all leaves and no fruit this year, switch to a fruit tree formula next season.

Q20. *Recognizing roses.* Can you identify a rose I saw and really want? It is a shrub type, with reddish leaves and flowers that are yellow, orange, and rosy pink all at the same time.

A20. Though I never claim to be psychic, I believe the rose you seek is known as the butterfly rose (*Rosa mutabilis*). A wonderful, nearly carefree garden shrub, each flower progresses through the colors with age, producing the tricolor effect you describe. I like its reddish new growth and flat-faced blossoms. If you like flowers that change with age, look for Yes- terday, Today and Tomorrow. This is not a rose, but *Brunfelsia australis*, a large tropical shrub that blooms well in containers. Its flowers open violet, then lighten to lavender, and are finally white. It's a beauty.

Q21. *Algae out of control.* My pond holds 150 gallons of water and I have two goldfish in it. The pump works fine and I love my lilies, but there's too much algae. What can I do? My friend suggests snails, but I don't really want to bring them into the garden.

A21. Snails wouldn't be my first choice to solve this dilemma. You need to understand that algae is primarily a function of sunlight. Remove its source and the algae won't grow. It's simply a matter of adding more floating plants to the pond, enough to cover two-thirds of the water surface. Water lettuce may be the fastest growing of the popular surface plants. It is the easiest to pull out when it's overgrown, and it's readily available.

Q22. *Landscaping a new home.* We're building a new home that won't be finished until summer. Can we sod then, or should we use seed because of the heat? We have an irrigation system, so watering shouldn't be a problem.

A22. If money is no object, I'd sod because the effect is immediate. However, you will need to water carefully to ensure success. If economy is

an issue, here's an idea: seed the backyard to prevent erosion and sod the front for great looks. Summer heat stress is a problem either way, and you will have to keep the seedbed or new sod evenly moist for at least a month to get the grass going.

Q23. *Scruffy wax myrtles.* Why do my wax myrtles look different from everyone else's? Theirs are thick trunked and almost trees, but mine are shrubby and have lots of suckers coming up everywhere.

A23. Like gangly teenagers, wax myrtles (*Myrica cerifera*) take a few years to get past the scruffy stages you describe. Be quick to snap off the suckers that appear and don't overfertilize with nitrogen. Use a balanced tree fertilizer if you feed at all. Trunks thicken with time and maturity.

Q24. *Aggravating azaleas.* I planted a hundred azaleas last year and they grew fine, but never made flowers this year. Do you know what happened and how I can prevent it next year?

A24. So long as the site for the azaleas has about half a day of sun, there are two likely causes for your problem: fertilizer and pruning. Perhaps you amended the bed with organic matter properly, but didn't use an azalea fertilizer on the plants—that would provide plenty of leaves but few flowers. Or perhaps you pruned them too late in the year and cut off the buds for this year. Fertilize this season and don't prune at all, then look for flowers next spring.

Q25. *Cultivating clematis.* Do you know how to propagate clematis vines? I like my friend's better than any I've seen and would like some of it. Is now the right time to take cuttings, or do I have to use seed?

the base is the clematis seed, life-size.

A25. Clematis seed require a conditioning process to prepare them to sprout. Mix fresh seed with a few spoonfuls of dampened vermiculite. Put the combinaton into a plastic container with a snap top, and set it in an unheated space, like your

garage or outdoor shed. Open it up and take a look at the seeds every week or so. It may take all winter for the seeds to sprout, but you'll see them poke that first root out eventually. Then lift them carefully and plant them into potting soil to grow until big enough to plant out. This process is long and drawn out (rather like this explanation) and isn't guaranteed to work or to produce the same clematis that produced the seed, since many are hybrids and do not 'come true' from seed. But cuttings taken from immature, soft stems in early summer should root quite easily in a mix of compost or good garden soil and sand. I take a six inch cutting, strip the leaves off the lower half, then stick the cutting into a quart sized pot. Grow it in the shade, keep it moist, and tug on the cutting in about a month. If it resists, you've got roots.

Q26. *Leafless azalea.* My wild azalea hasn't leafed out yet. Should I dig it up or try and fertilize it to see if it'll grow again?

A26. I once transplanted a native azalea from the wild and it took two years to recover, so don't lose hope yet. Use the thumbnail scratch test first to see if there's any green left under the bark. Start out on the twigs and scrape off a thin bit of bark. If they're brown, scratch the branch behind the twigs, and so forth until you find green tissue. Once you determine that the shrub is still alive, cut back any dead branches then fertilize and water to see if new growth will emerge. If that doesn't work, dig it up and move it to a more suitable location—some shade and an organic soil that stays moist between waterings.

Q27. *Awful armadillos.* There are armadillos digging up my lawn and I don't want to shoot them. Do you have any ideas for running them off?

A27. Traditional wisdom says they're looking for food and you've got it, so there they are. Armadillos are more opportunistic than moles and other digging vermin—it's not just your garden they want. They'll walk a mile for a bowl of pet food or overripe fruit sitting on top of the compost pile. Clean up your area, and hope your armadillo isn't a female— once they've had a litter in your garage, they get territorial and may have to be trapped and hauled away.

Q28 _Problems with amaryllis._

I planted the amaryllis bulb I got for Christmas two years ago into the garden, but it has never bloomed. I feed it every year with blood meal. What else can I do?

A28. Your choice of fertilizer

supplies mostly nitrogen, the element that induces great green leaves, so it's working! But now you need to add potassium and phosphorus to encourage flowering. Use a bulb food, or any granular flower "bloomer" formula this year.

Photo courtesy of Park Seed

Q29. _Heightening a hedge._ Do you have an idea for me to speed

up a hedge? I bought a house and there's privet and eleagnus between me and the road, but it's wimpy. How often can I fertilize them?

A29. If I had a choice, I wouldn't use either of these as a sheared

hedge, but unless you want to start again from scratch, here's what to do. Start now to grow a thick hedge by pruning and fertilizing in sequence through the growing season. Cut the bushes back by about one-third now and feed with a balanced shrub formula. Keep them watered so the fertilizer can get to the roots and watch for new shoots along the old stems and on top. In June, cut a few inches off the top and fertilize with a nitrogen source like cottonseed meal. At mid-August, prune to shape the new growth and even up the hedge, then use a 'winterizer' formula on them. Follow these instructions, and in a couple of years the hedge will be huge and thick.

Q30. _Miserable mexican heather._ I bought Mexican heather

last year and was told it is perennial, but it never came back up. What's wrong—my growing techniques or the information?

A30. If you live in an area with no frost all winter, Mexican

heather (_Cuphea hyssopifolia_) will return reliably; otherwise, treat any regrowth as a happy surprise. Cupheas are native to tropical and subtropical regions of the Western Hemisphere where they are perennial.

Q31. *Trials of the trellis.*
Everything I've planted on my trellis dies just when I need the shade of its leaves. I've tried morning glory and hyacinth bean vines. Both did well for awhile, but didn't last all summer or reseed themselves as I'd hoped. Is there another kind of plant I could try?

A31.
I'd forget the annuals for this purpose and go for a woody vine like akebia (chocolate vine) that keeps its leaves all summer. Yours may also be a perfect spot for *Rosa* 'Lady Banks'. This species blooms but once in spring, but provides a dense leaf cover that is nearly evergreen in most areas and has no thorns (so you can train its vigorous canes more easily). The traditional flower color is yellow, but the white variety has more fragrance.

Q32. *Rooting bridal wreath spirea.*
I'd like to have some of the bridal wreath spirea at my aunt's house. How can I root some, or is there another way to go?

A32.
This great plant is a southern classic, but dividing may be the way to go. If you look underneath your aunt's shrubs, you'll likely see small plants sprouted from the roots. Use a sharpshooter shovel (that long, very narrow type) to dig up several, slicing right through to take up roots and the above-ground stems together. Then pot them up, cut back the stems to about a foot tall, and keep them watered and fertilized until you can plant them next fall. Or, take six inch cuttings in July, and root in a small pot of moist sand and compost. Water sparingly, but mist the pots several times a day until roots form in a few weeks. It's tricky, but can be done.

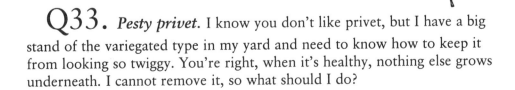

Q33. *Pesty privet.*
I know you don't like privet, but I have a big stand of the variegated type in my yard and need to know how to keep it from looking so twiggy. You're right, when it's healthy, nothing else grows underneath. I cannot remove it, so what should I do?

A33. My objection to Japanese privet is twofold: first, it is a haven for whiteflies, and if they live there, it's a short hop to more desirable plants. Second, because it is easily spread, this invader has overrun whole areas of our region, shading out our native woodland plants. But at least the variegated form offers color, and I understand the dilemma of removing it from an established landscape. Give it grudging focal point status for its color, and surround it with red cypress mulch. I'd also suggest pruning it severely in early spring to stimulate new growth lower down on the plant, then trimming off the flowers as soon as they appear just as you would the bloom clusters on Japanese ligustrum to reduce irritating pollen and seed production.

Q34. *Identifying trees.* Can you give me some information about a huge tree I saw? It has big lavender flowers and is called royal something or other. Can I get one for my front yard?

A34. I think you've seen royal paulownia (*P. tomentosa*) and it is an unusual tree, but not suitable for most front gardens. The problem is, the tree drops its leaves during summer and fall, and each fruit has more than a thousand winged seeds that then sprout wherever they drop. This is too much litter for most folks to deal with in such a prominent setting.

Q35. *Pruning privet hedge.* How far back can I cut a ligustrum hedge? We just moved into an older home and the hedge is ten feet tall with leaves only at the top.

A35. You can cut that hedge back by half in late winter or very early spring, fertilize it, and expect a fair amount of new growth in the first year that will be thicker at the bottom since that's all you'll leave. But

if the landscape can benefit from a different look, prune up instead of down for a tree form. Clip all the branches off that are below head-height to create an overhead canopy, then plant small shrubs underneath if the area needs a low hedge to screen a view. Those treeform ligustrums will offer height, interesting trunks, and could cost more than $100 each if you decided to buy some!

Q36. *Planting Bermudagrass sod.* We built a new home last fall and put out ryegrass seed to keep the ground from eroding. When can I plant Bermudagrass sod and how do I take care of it?

A36. Good for you to get that ground covered before the rainy season—you don't want to lose what you've got! Install the sod once all danger of frost has passed in your area. First, mow down the rye and rake or till the area so it is smooth as if you were planting seed. Remember, lumps and holes now will be lumps and holes in your lawn, so do the soil prep work and plant carefully to make a smooth surface before buying the sod. Be sure to watch for 'knitting' whether you sod yourself or hire someone. Be sure to watch for 'knitting' whether you do it yourself or hire someone. Each piece of sod must be fitted neatly (or knitted as it's called) so there will be no gaps between pieces, and no hills and valleys in your lawn.

Q37. *Suitable seed names.* What is the real name of a big seed my friend gave me? She called it monkey balls but I'm sure it has another name I can give to my garden club when I recommend it.

A37. Yes, it does. The heart-shaped leaves of *Discorea bulbifera* and the tubers it produces in the leaf axils give rise to many common names, including the one you find inappropriate for some ears. Call it 'tater vine' or 'air potato' and no one will blush.

Q38. *Fierce fire ants.* For the last two years, fire ants have invaded my vegetable patch and have nearly run me out, not to mention ruining some plants. Can I treat them if I'm going to eat what grows there?

A38. Not with the most effective fire ant treatments, which are baits meant to be distributed across the entire area that the worker ants patrol for food each day. Here's what I do when a mound appears in the vegetable garden: first, put a baited control out in the lawn or perimeter of your garden. Then treat that mound with something that will run them off but will not persist in the soil such as blood meal or even boiling water. Dump it right on the mound, then water steadily until drenched. Next day, take a stiff rake and knock down the mound. Likely the ants will set up shop a few feet away in the lawn or an ornamental bed. Then you can treat with a contact insecticide or wait for the bait to take them out.

Q39. *Surprise plants.* I want to plant a surprise for my wife, who is coming home in a few weeks after several months in the hospital. We have a three-tier octagon shaped bed and I need some ideas. I've made good soil for it as you instructed (potting soil, compost, etc.) and want some plant suggestions. I can water it easily and it's in nearly full sun. What would you plant?

A39. What a fine welcome home gift! Since you don't specify a type of plant, my choices are to use a combination of shrubs, annual flowers, and vegetables. Put a tomato or two in the top tier with a cage around it to hold the plants high up. Or choose a short canna lily like 'Bengal Tiger' if she's not a 'mater fan. Then encircle the second tier with a single type of dwarf shrub, so it's consistently attractive. Choose from nandina, spirea, dwarf barberry (*Berberis* 'Crimson Pygmy'), or juniper (*Juniperus* 'Bar Harbor'). Plant perennials such as stokes' aster (*Stokesia*) or bugleweed (*Ajuga reptans*) between the shrubs and add some variegated ivy, too. Use annuals in the lower tier for a cut flower bouquet: petunias, zinnias, celosia, little dahlias, and coleus would make a colorful start.

Q40. *Weather-wilted tomatoes.* What would make 'Patio' tomatoes wilt at the top every day? I have them in full sun on the deck in big pots and really want to get some fruit. The leaves look fine, just wilted by the time I come home.

A40. If no other damage is present, the leaves are not chewed or twisted, turning brown or falling off, I think better water management will easily solve your problem. Water every morning. Be sure to fill the pots with water, let it drain out, then fill them again to the top of the pot before you leave for the day. If you cannot do that, get a water-holding product (usually a gel-like substance that is clear and gritty when dry, and

expands greatly when wet) from the local garden store and add that to the pot. If you look at plants in public places like malls, you'll often see it used to maintain the plants between visits from the caretakers. Don't overdo it—a little goes a long way with this material.

Q41. *Other uses for a hose-end sprayer.* I got a sprayer with
some fertilizer that goes on the end of my hose. I've used up the fertilizer and want to know what else I can use this sprayer for. Can I put weed killer in it and spray my lawn?

A41. Hose-end sprayers are very handy and can
be used for just about any product that must be diluted before application. But understand that no sprayer should be used for both herbicides and other products because the fittings may hold some of the weed killer, and such substances can damage the plants you're trying to help. My advice is to get two sprayers, then label and use them separately—one for weed killers and the other for fertilizers and pesticides.

Q42. *Hibiscus bloom.* When do
perennial hibiscus start blooming? I planted three two years ago and they bloomed fine, but haven't since. I feed them with 8-8-8 and cut them back after the tops die down. What am I doing wrong?

A42. I'd stay on the same track, but
change the engine. Use a perennial flowering formula fertilizer instead of the agriculture standard, 8-8-8. Look for a formula you can work into the soil around the plants with an analysis such as 5-10-10. You'll get less leaf and more stems and flowers when you reduce the nitrogen (the first number in the formula).

Q43. *Deer repellant.* I planted my first garden last fall (lettuce, greens, and broccoli) but the deer ate most of it. Is there a repellant product that really works, and won't harm my vegetables?

A43. Most of the repellants are not toxic, but they don't always run the hungry deer off, either. If you live near woods or the natural range of a herd, they'll just wait you out. Folks try hanging bars of soap on the plants, putting motion detector lights in the garden, and spraying all sorts of products, with varying results. For the money and time you'll spend doing all that (not to mention how weird the garden looks with soap on a rope everywhere), build a fence around the garden patch. That will send the deer elsewhere, and the bunnies, too.

Chapter 4
Deep South Summer
July, August, September

~~~~~~~*Summer in the Garden* ~~~~~~~

If there were such a thing as a southern thesaurus, you'd find these synonyms for summer: sultry, languid, sticky, and oppressive. Hot and humid doesn't begin to describe it most days, and some nights, throughout the region. When nights reach into the seventies, beans can't bloom and tomatoes won't set fruit. Vicious mosquitoes are most active at dawn and dusk, so even those times aren't great for garden chores. People who live in the South endure between 70 and 120 days a year above 86 degrees, and temperatures above 100 are annual features anywhere south of Memphis.

Watch the dewpoint (the temperature, humidity, and atmospheric pressure at which dew forms), for when the nighttime low temperature and the dewpoint converge, there's hope for a thunderstorm. Plants love these conditions, and to tell the truth, so do I. We walk and talk slower, but plants grow faster and that's joy to a gardener. There's nothing better than elephant ears and canna lilies with leaves as big as your arms. Southern summers deliver the goods.

Annual flowers and vines. Water baskets and pots daily in hot weather, or add a few crystals of a water-holding material to the soil. Fill pots with ice cubes for a slow soak and to limit runoff onto patios and porches.

Trim back leggy petunias, impatiens, and vinca—use scissors, hedge shears, or even a string trimmer for large plantings—so they can bush out again and bloom til frost. Fertilize with organic nitrogen such as cottonseed meal, water well, and follow up with a balanced fertilizer in ten days.

Great Summer Annuals

bacopa (Sutera grandiflora)

fanflower (Scaveola aemula)

impatiens (I. wallerana)

zinnia, classic and narrow-leaf (Z. elegans, Z. angustifolia)

petunia 'Wave' series

surfinias (such as 'Million Bells')

celosias: chenille, feather, and cockscomb

coleus

cleome

melampodium (M. paludosum 'Derby' and others)

purple fountain grass (Pennisetum setaceum 'Rubrum')

Questions and Answers for Deep South Gardeners

Start seedlings for transplant next month: poppies, larkspur, violas, snapdragons, and stock. Fill a flat with peat based potting soil or soil starting mix, water it once, then scatter seed evenly and cover lightly with more soil. Use a watering can with a rosehead to keep the flat moist daily, or lay a piece of wood over the soil to retain moisture. Lift it each day, water if needed, and remove completely as soon as the seeds sprout.

Trees and shrubs. That light mist you feel while standing under river birch, crape myrtle, or other trees isn't rain. Piercing and sucking insects like aphids and whiteflies stay busy dehydrating their succulent leaves all summer. The mist comes from the "honeydew" they secrete. Spray insecticidal soap with pyrethrin weekly while insects are present, or use a systemic insecticide once when they first appear.

Junipers, spruce, and other needle-leafed evergreens can develop branches that look almost burned—they turn reddish brown and eventually drop off entirely. Spider mites are the culprit here; prune off the damaged areas since they will not recover. Then dispose of them to reduce reinfestation. Spray with a miticide if symptoms return, for other pesticides are ineffective against spider mites.

> TIP: Spider mites thrive in hot, dry conditions. Wind a soaker hose through plantings of groundcover juniper, lantana, verbena and other susceptible plants, then turn it on daily just long enough to disrupt them.

Stressed trees will drop small branches, shed leaves prematurely, and attract lichen, a harmless but some say unattractive fungus that usually looks like gray lace along a narrow branch. Prune out the lichen if you wish, mulch around the tree, and water it regularly.

Herbs and vegetables. In early summer, plant pumpkin seeds in hills for jack-o-lanterns by Halloween. First work up a space about two feet square and six to eight inches deep in a vegetable row or the edge of a flowerbed. Add compost or leaf mold to the native soil to improve drainage and a little manure to fertilize the vines. Make a 'hill' of the cultivated soil (though it won't be more than two inches high). Dig a hole on one side of the hill and sink a coffee can pierced with holes around the bottom for a reservoir of water and plant food. Sow four seeds in each hill with plenty of room between, at least four feet along the row, then thin to two plants. Keep the reservoir full of water and soluble fertilizer all the time, for pumpkins are heavy feeders and thirsty besides.

86

BUSHY PERENNIALS

Pinch back tips of fall-blooming perennials until July Fourth. This keeps chrysanthemums, asters, goldenrod, and joe pye weed short and bushy. Plants will have more flowers and need less staking.

Keep harvesting hot peppers. Make a deliciously spicy vinegar from a selection of tabasco, jalapeno, cayenne, and chili peppers, or whichever types you like. Use a clean jar or bottle. Take off the stems and put the peppers in whole, then fill the container with cider vinegar, covering the peppers completely. Let it steep for a week before using. It is excellent on field peas and cabbage. But beware, if it sits around and steeps, this brew can get fiery!

As the season moves on, start planting seeds of fall vegetables and herbs. Leafy greens like mustard, spinach, turnips, collards, swiss chard, and mesclun grow best under floating row covers. Broccoli and cabbage can be seeded directly, but in the warmest areas, provide a bit of shade and daily water for the new seedlings.

Perennial flowers and vines. Give less-than-great perennials a summer boost with a light application of timed-release perennial fertilizer, composted manure, or organic fertilizer such as kelp or fish emulsion. Prune off any dead stems or leaves, remove spent flowers, and add new mulch to renew them.

Locate and eradicate ragweed and goldenrod if allergies trouble you. Both are a source of pollen that can reach you from the garden, though goldenrod at a distance is a beautiful part of the late summer landscape.

Divide and relocate all the daisies: ox-eye, shastas, and 'May Queen' will not bloom if crowded together in tight clumps. Dig up a shovelful of the clump, then cut it apart. Don't tear the plants or risk damaging the roots and crown because these are essential elements for viability.

Bulbs. Divide bearded iris to prevent borers in crowded stands. Replant the largest clumps on top of the soil— just nestle the rhizomes in, with half their surface showing above ground. Cut leaves into a fan for easy handling and less transplant shock.

TIP: Keep mesh onion and orange bags around for use later. They are excellent for dry storage of bulbs. Use sawdust or peatmoss to overwinter caladium, 'tater vine, and dahlia where you cannot leave these bulbs in the soil.

Remove spent flower stalks of daylilies, crinium, amaryllis, gladiolas, nile lilies, and crocosmia. All can be dug, divided, and replanted now, or put in containers to share or carry over for a new garden bed this fall.

Once caladiums begin to lose their luster, or make repeated attempts to bloom,

87

they're headed downhill. Dig them up while you can still see which variety is which, and label them! Rub, don't wash, the dirt off the tubers, cut the leaves down, and store bulbs dry over the winter in paper sacks.

BANANA PUDDING

Line a glass 8x8 pan with vanilla wafers, bottom and sides. Add layers of bananas, then wafers. Pour on some vanilla pudding, freshly cooked and still warm. Add more layers and pudding until the pan is full. Top with vanilla wafers and refrigerate overnight. Just before serving, make a meringue of egg whites beaten until stiff with sugar. Pile it high on top of the pudding and brown in a hot oven (450 degrees). Serve right away.

Groundcovers and lawns. Even if you miss a week, don't cut off more than a third of the grass height at one time. The combination of summer's heat and excess leaf loss can cause stress that lasts for months. Mow again in a few days to catch up. And if you usually bag the clippings, leave a layer on the lawn at least once this summer instead, to recycle their nutrients.

There's still time to push groundcovers to fill the spaces between young plants. Pull back the mulch and water each plant thoroughly with soluble fertilizer. This can be applied using a hose-end sprayer which works well for large areas. This method of applying fertilizer will reach the leaves of your plants where it will be absorbed and will benefit the plant almost as much as the nutrients it receives from the soil.

Control weeds in the lawn by hand whenever possible. But if half the turf has disappeared under the weeds, consider spraying with a broadleaf weed control product designed for your weeds and your lawn type. Take a piece of each to the garden center if you're not certain.

Fruit. Once the strawberry harvest is complete, take care of the mother plants to encourage their survival and multiplication. Fertilize plants with an organic nitrogen like cottonseed meal or fish emulsion. Replace the straw beneath them to give emerging runners room to grow. Watch for chewed leaves and other signs of insects; if they cannot be controlled, discard the plants and start again in the fall.

Put on long sleeves one more time and get blackberries ready for a surge of new canes and leaves this season. Pinch the tips off young plants to force branching. Cut back good-looking canes to 40 inches tall. But remove old canes entirely to make room for the new ones.

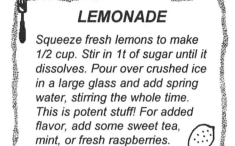

LEMONADE

Squeeze fresh lemons to make 1/2 cup. Stir in 1t of sugar until it dissolves. Pour over crushed ice in a large glass and add spring water, stirring the whole time. This is potent stuff! For added flavor, add some sweet tea, mint, or fresh raspberries.

Keep the fall fruits watered to promote a sweet, good textured harvest. Pears, persimmons, and pecans are not drought tolerant. If they begin to lose leaves before the fruit is mature, they won't develop and you'll lose the crop.

Plants in pots. Houseplants such as ficus, dracaena, Chinese evergreen, etc., thrive on summer's humidity in a shady spot outside. But they look like lunch to many insects. Repot them when they are too crowded (if they wilt only a few hours after they are watered, it may be a sign that they need bigger pots), or if a pot falls over with too much top growth for its size. Keep the plants watered, fertilize twice a month, and watch for signs of insects so you can control them quickly.

Fill outdoor containers with mums and asters. When shopping, look for small plants not yet in bloom. Not only are they economical, but small plants provide good, fast growth, and, often, the widest selection of flower types. Choose colors to complement or contrast with your garden's theme, or show your team spirit with mums that match the football team's jersey.

~~~~~~~ Growing notes ~~~~~~~

Weed control. Weeds are the great equalizer of gardening—everybody must deal with them sooner or later. To make matters worse, their numbers increase exponentially just when temperatures warm up. So there  you have the most necessary and unpleasant of summer garden chores. Any plant growing out of place meets the gardener's definition of a weed. Use a combination of force, mulch, solarization, and as a last resort, a chemical spray to get them out of the way. Pull them up, or hoe, till and rake them out, and then mulch the area to deprive them of sun and water. Glyphosate weed control products seem to me to be the most useful and least intrusive to the environment when a chemical control becomes necessary. Three points to remember: 1) that glyphosate has the potential to damage or kill any green tissue it reaches, 2) that new growth and warm weather are your allies when using chemical weed controls or solarization, and 3) a daily walk with hoe in hand may be the best form of weed control you can practice.

Bagworms and webworms. An assortment of insects protect their feeding habits and lifestyles by surrounding their vulnerable bodies with webs or bags. Such webs are often formed by excreting a sticky or silklike substance The webs shed rainfall and insecticide sprays with ease, but physical controls will usually solve the problem, at least for the season. You can puncture and pluck off the bags with a long stick or a broom wrapped in cheesecloth. Most of the time, these pests are uglier than they are dangerous.

time to deadhead

Deadheading flowers. Widely known as the way to keep annuals blooming, cutting blooms off before they fade completely (deadheading) can also promote the rebloom of some perennials, shrubs, and even trees like crape myrtle (*Lagerstromia indica*). In most cases, make the cut down the stem from the withered flower, just above the first set of good leaves.

Storing annual seed. Once your open-pollinated annual flowers and vegetables have gone to seed, you can save seeds to grow and share that will 'come true,' that is, be exactly like their parent plant. Though most hybrid seeds may not come true, their results can be fun to grow and who knows? You may find the next wildly popular plant among your seedlings.

Let the seed pods of flowers dry completely on the plant unless overwhelming amounts of rain threaten them with mold. Then cut the seed-bearing stems when they are as dry as possible, and let the seeds continue to dry indoors. The structures around the seeds will begin to open as they dry. You can then rub or shake them out. Separate the chaff by hand-cleaning or screening.

To store seed from a moist environment like the inside of a tomato, let the fruit ripen fully on the plant, then cut it open and scoop out the seed onto a paper towel. Rinse the seeds gently in water to separate them, then lay them on another paper towel to dry. Store annual seeds in plain white paper envelopes (label them first!). Put a bunch of the white envelopes in a zippered plastic bag and store them in the refrigerator or even a desk drawer, but never in the freezer.

Fern care. When hot nights and days conspire against ferns in baskets and pots, give them the bucket cure. Fern rootballs can be very tight masses, and water often pours right through. That's fine when conditions are moderate, but in summer ferns can dehydrate badly, turn a pale shade of green, and stop growing. Submerge the entire container in a tub of tepid water with a half strength solution of a balanced, soluble fertilizer (look for even numbers on the label, such as 20-20-20). Leave it there for two to three hours for maximum soaking. Then hang it up in bright but not direct sunlight.

Rooting shrub cuttings. When the wood of many favorite shrubs no longer bends easily, but doesn't yet snap at your touch, it is semi-mature, or semihard, and at an excellent for propagation with cuttings. Nandina, snowball viburnum, hydrangea, kerria, and camellia are just some examples. Take a six-inch cutting and strip the leaves off the lower half, then stick into a mix of damp sand and peat based potting soil. Lots of gardeners dip the end of the cutting into a rooting hormone powder, just for insurance. Keep the pot moist in a humid spot that is out of direct sunlight to promote rooting.

Choosing a sprayer. Pressure sprayers that pump up, handheld squirt bottles, hose-end attachments—each type of sprayer has its place. To simply add humidity to indoor plants or to mix and spray small amounts of chemicals, a small squirt bottle can fill the bill quite simply. For larger jobs, pressure sprayers and hose-end types offer two different kinds of spray. The small nozzles of pressure sprayers are adjustable, and the pressure you pump into the tank makes it easy to control where the spray falls. Hose-ends take advantage of water pressure to distribute larger amounts of chemical fertilizer or pesticide at one time. If you spray both pesticides and herbicides, keep your plants safe by getting two sprayers so you don't apply weedkiller on them by accident. Use a permanent marker to put a huge H on the one for herbicide.

~~~~Smart Gardening ~~~~

Water. Few garden beliefs are as true as this one: plants grow better if you provide water in ample amounts and timely fashion. That said, here's the lowdown on how to water without drowning either your plants or your wallet. Garden plants fall generally into three categories: water lovers (bog and pond plants), water shirkers (cacti, succulents, and epiphytes), and moderate drinkers. The majority of garden plants fall into the third group.

They need enough water weekly to irrigate their rootzone and time enough between applications to dry out slightly. This should not cause wilting.

The books say 'an inch a week' but take that as a guide, for an inch in your garden is not the same as a rain gauge measure or weather service report. A downpour from the skies may register ample amounts, but its rapid rate means most of the water runs off, and not into, the garden beds. Likewise, afternoon spot showers may add up to an inch weekly without ever truly watering the garden. Don't depend on rain to water your garden!

The ideal watering system for me is one that you can turn on and off at will, with minimal hose dragging and sprinkler setting. That means being ready to water before the need arises, by knowing your own soil and plants. In order to do this, you must make a plan and use it. Inground irrigation systems, soaker hoses, sprinklers positioned for ready use, or a well-wielded watering can and hose with a fan nozzle——you pick the method, then monitor its use. Trust me, this equipment pays off when you arrive home some hot July afternoon when it hasn't rained for ten days. The plants on which you have invested your time and energy wilt along with your spirits. All you have to do to alleviate these summer garden blues is turn on the water system.

TOP TEN (PLUS ONE) VEGETABLES

to plant from summer into fall (in order of planting)

1. Pumpkins—plant seed in hills, but form low reservoirs in the soil nearby to feed the big hungry vines

2. Southern peas—your choice: crowders, ladypeas, silverskins, purplehulls, and field peas

3. Tomatoes—keep old vines going, root new cuttings, or start new plants for the fall crop in July

4. Squash—fall crops avoid the aphids that trouble spring plantings

5. Bush beans—plant now, harvest til frost, then dig in the vines for organic matter

6. Broccoli and cabbage—start seeds right away, or transplant in August; water daily

7. Collards, cauliflower, and Brussels sprouts—shade your transplants to prevent wilt and stunting

8. Spinach, leaf lettuces, and Swiss chard—plant seed, then thin to stand four inches apart

9. Potatoes—plant whole, small potatoes for this season, preferably some you saved from earlier crops

10. Garlic, parsley, cilantro—plant these herbs in September for spring harvests

11. Carrots, turnips, and beets—plant seed in very loose soil, thin to three inches apart on all sides

Apply water slowly so it soaks into the bed without excess runoff. Poke around in the bed as you irrigate to see how wet the soil actually gets. You may be amazed by how much water never makes it past the mulch—be sure it does. Soaker hoses under the mulch make that incredibly easy to do and those made from recycled tires (they're usually black, round and rough to the touch) literally leak from their entire surface directly into the soil. Even if you don't care about the environmental benefits of using them, soakers will save you money. I tend just over an acre of land, about one third of it in beds with soakers. In converting those areas from sprinklers a few years ago, I cut my water bills in half, even after the municipality raised its rates by a third!

I use hoses with sprinklers or fan nozzles in some situations. For example, they are fine for watering the lawn during times of drought, or irrigating beds of annuals . But I keep old-fashioned watering cans with rose nozzles handy for smaller tasks like watering seedlings, spot watering of the occasional wilted plant, and applying soluble fertilizers.

Watering more deeply but less often encourages deep rooting of plants. That in turn gives them more staying power to withstand other changing conditions of weather, fertility, and wind. Don't forget about fertilizer, soil preparation, and plant selection appropriate for your site, but know that water makes the difference in all of them.

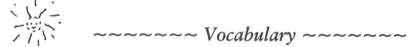

~~~~~~~ *Vocabulary* ~~~~~~~

Solarization. The use of the power of sunlight and heat to suppress weeds and insects in garden soil will amaze even theose skeptical of traditional organic practices. It works by focusing the sun's rays onto the soil through clear plastic coverings for a period of weeks or even months. Solarization is non toxic to the environment (unless you're a weed seed) and often just as effective as other forms of weed control.

Parasite. These are bad boys—plants that attach themselves to another 'host' plant and can suck the life out of their hosts. Unlike some orchids and bromeliads that attach to other plants only for support, parasites such as dodder and mistletoe must have the host's nutrients to survive.

Side-dress. Think of this process as a targeted boost to extend or complete the season. Once corn is knee high, tomatoes have set their first fruits, or melons have their first flowers, these heavy feeders need more fertilizer placed in the soil alongside their stems. Just scratch in granular fertilizer or use soluble fertilizers according to package directions.

Dieback. As the name implies, this plant problem causes a branch to expire while the rest of the tree or shrub looks fine. The affected part just turns brown and often shrivels, but note that it does not look singed (then the trouble is fireblight). Prune out the damage, making the last cut in healthy wood about an inch below the damaged area.

Ergonomic adaptations. Anybody who has ever planted six flats of annuals and felt a stiff wrist or back for the next week needs to know about ergonomic tools and handles. Thanks to the latest in technology, tool design is taking the pressure off overworked muscles and relieving repetitive motion stress. Ergonomic tools may look funny to some, but so did telephones at first.

Fireblight. I first saw fireblight, a bacterial disease, on a pear tree. It also affects apple, a pyracantha, quince, and loquat, and, more rarely, Indian hawthorne or red-top photinia. One whole branch looks as if somebody took a flame thrower to it. Leaves still cling to branches; both are burned red to bronze to black. The best hope of controlling it is constant pruning back below the damage. Cut off the damaged branches when they first appear. To prevent spreading it with your tools, keep a cup of bleach handy and dip your shears between cuts. Future damage can be lessened by spraying the plant with copper sulfate several times next year, beginning as soon the flower buds develop color.

.......SUMMER QUESTIONS

Q1. *Tomato problem.* I have plenty of tomatoes, but they aren't right. The skins are thicker than they should be and they have black spots on the bottoms. I don't know how to solve the problem. Can you help me?

A1. You actually have two different problems that are related to your watering practices (or lack thereof). The black spots, known as blossom end rot, happen when water is not consistently available to the plants. They are dry one day and flooded the next. Thick skins often result from a lack of water during ripening. Solve both problems with more regular watering, and also apply mulch to keep the soil moist for a longer time; it helps prevent evaporation.

Q2. *Wind-damaged pines.* A strong wind came through and

damaged my pine trees, so I had them cut down. The workmen ground the stumps out and I tilled in the shavings. I want to plant a shade tree that will grow fairly fast. What do you suggest?

A2. The dilemma of planting replacement shade trees comes to this:

fast-growing trees don't always live forever. My solution is simple. Plant a combination of trees—some that will grow rapidly to provide shade sooner and others that will eventually grow huge and will be long lived. In the first category, look at tulip poplar (*Liriodendron tulipifera*), green ash (*Fraxinus pennsylvanica*), bald cypress (*Taxodium distichum*), overcup oak (*Quercus lyrata*), and water oak (*Q. nigra*). Luckily, the overcup and bald cypress are long-lived, too, but don't overlook the dawn redwood (*Metasequoia glypto-stroboides*) and the ginkgo (*G. biloba*).

Q3. *Dichondra distinction.* I moved from California to

Mississippi, and I recognize some plants in my new location but not others. I have a plant I thought was dichondra, but now I'm not sure. It's got round leaves but they're big and shinier than I'd expected, and now it's running all through the garden bed. What is it?

A3. The dichondra you speak of is used as a lawn substitute in some

places. But it's usually seen growing as one of many broadleaf 'weeds' in a lawn or the wet area where grass won't grow. You have dollar weed (*Hydrocotyle rotundifolia*, also called pennywort) and it's a big problem for many gardeners. Pull it out where you can, and dig up all the white runners you can find. Then, as it resprouts, use a glyphosate weed control product, but remember that these glyphosates will kill or damage anything green you spray. Crush the dollar leaves first with your hand so the chemical can be absorbed efficiently. Once the plants turn yellow, rip them out and mulch the bed. Always shield desirable plants from weed control products.

Q4. *Vegetables gone yellow.* Some of my vegetables have gone

yellow all over, especially the beans. Should I fertilize?

A4. Not the beans, please. If they're yellow, they're done, so turn

them into the soil to capture their nutrients and great organic matter. Other summer vegetables could use frequent dose of fertilizer. In fact, if more than a couple of leaves at the bottom have turned yellow, you're late.

Q5. *Falling squash.* Why do the little squash drop off my plants?

A5. Early in the season, female plants put on little squashes. If they're not pollinated, and often the male flowers open a bit too late, the squashes fall off. You may choose to grab a paintbrush, dip it in the pollen and transfer it yourself to be sure the job's done. If the plants have been bearing and then begin dropping fruit, be sure you're watering and fertilizing enough to keep up with their growth and the squash production, or the plant won't be able to ripen the bounty.

Q6. *Black bananas.* What is the black coating on my banana shrub? Almost every leaf has it and I'm afraid it will kill the bush.

A6. Your shrubs have sooty mold, a well-named fungus disease that also affects gardenias and crape myrtles in too many gardens. The problem is, the fungus grows in honeydew secreted by insects who stay busy piercing and sucking your plants. So you must control the insects to control the sooty mold. First, wash it off with soapy water in a hose-end sprayer. Then use your choice of insecticidal soap, pyrethrin, or, in serious cases, a granular systemic insecticide. When such a fungus is a problem on the same plants for more than two seasons, it's serious. Choose a systemic insecticide that targets the insect you have, and is effective with only annual or semi-annual applications.

Q7. *Lemon argument.* Please settle an argument. My husband gave me a lemon tree in a big pot and I just love it. The flowers smelled great and now it has lemons on it. He says they'll turn yellow and I say they won't. Who's right?

A7. Lemons (*Citrus limon*) will bloom and fruit off and on through the year when grown in a warm, humid setting. In fact, most unripened fruit is the same color as the ripened fruit on the same tree, so it can be difficult to tell which of the fruits may be ready. It all depends on what variety of lemon you have. 'Meyer' is bright, dark yellow, while 'Ponderosa' is a much lighter color and looks more like a grapefruit. 'Lisbon' and 'Eureka' fall somewhere in

between, and there are other lemons with nearly orange and nearly green mature fruit. In general, once the fruits have stopped increasing in size, they begin to ripen rapidly. Start tasting in about two weeks; if the taste isn't quite right to you, try again in another week. Once harvested, lemons will store for about a month—keep them dry and cool to retain their good taste.

Q8. *Vine identification.* There's a vine growing through the fence that I think is poison ivy, but the guy next door says it's Virginia creeper. I want to pull it off my side, but don't want to touch it if it's poison. How can I tell?

A8. Either way, pulling won't stop those vines from regrowing on the fence if your neighbor doesn't work with you to accomplish physical and/or chemical removal. Virginia creeper (*Parthenocissus quinquefolia*) has five fingered leaflets, red new growth, and dark green leaves all summer. Poison ivy (*Rhus radicans*) has three leaflet leaves in various arrangements of lobes, but generally is lighter green than creeper and turns red in fall. In general, 'leaves of three, let it be.' However, the two vines often cohabit, so use care in both cases.

Q9. *Big bad beavers.* We built a new house in a lovely area near a lake with woods nearby. We planted ten trees and beavers have stripped the bark off six of them since last year. What can we do?

A9. Move before they start on the porch! Yours is one of the problems common to new construction in areas where wild creatures are displaced by development. The beavers (and other wildlife in other areas) were there first and will try to stay. Wrap undamaged tree trunks with hardware cloth or other wire to deter chewing, and be glad you don't have a stream for them to dam up. Of course, you could take the ancient approach to dealing with critters in the home garden—build a fence around all the land you plan to tend. That's what a 'garden' is, a sheltered, 'guarded' space between the house and the wild areas beyond it.

Q10. *Ugly lawn needs help.* My lawn looks terrible and I think it's the soil since weeds don't even grow in the bare spots. Do you have any ideas for improving the situation?

A10. If the lawn gets plenty of sunlight and water, but bare spots remain, compaction is often the problem. Soils collapse under the constant weight and pressure of construction machinery, traffic, playground areas, and the dog's run along the fence. Plants cannot grow, and dead zones result. But bare spots can also be the result of chemical spills, lawn scalpings, and outdoor furniture. Fido can cause trouble spots, too, if he uses one area too often. Use a stiff rake to work up the spots, topdress with an inch of compost and work that in before replanting or seeding some new grass. Keep reworked areas watered well until established.

Q11. *Zucchini problems.* I love zucchini and planted three hills this year. They did fine for awhile and the zucchini was delicious, but recently I noticed the plants have wilted. I watered them plenty, but they never perked back up. What went wrong?

A11. Overnight wilting in squash or pumpkins is a dramatic sign of squash vine borers, and a fatal one. If you cut into one of the stems, you'll likely find the culprit. But it's too late to do anything about it, although sometimes a longitudinal slit through the stem and the borer larva can save the plant. Next time you grow squash, watch for mother moth to flit about laying amber colored eggs on the undersides of leaves and scrape them off, or drop a floating grow cover over the whole plant to protect it.

Q12. *Pale bird of paradise.* My friend brought back a bird of paradise plant from a trip and gave it to me when it started looking pale at her house. How do I take care of it?

A12. Grow bird of paradise (*Strelitzia* species) as a tropical container plant. Be aware that temperatures below 30 degrees damage them or kill them outright. Give your plant a peat-based potting soil amended with a cup of compost per gallon of potting soil, very bright light, and water when the top inch of soil feels dry (stick your finger in it to test). Fertilize often. It is a fast grower if you feed it regularly. And don't be quick to repot since crowded roots promote flowers for this plant.

Q13. *Big butterfly bushes.* How big do butterfly bushes get? The one I planted last summer is now over six feet tall. It's blooming but not as much as last year. Can I prune it to get more flowers?

A13. Yes, and you should do it right away. Midsummer pruning for many butterfly bushes (*Buddleia* species) seems to benefit them in the long run. Clipping off the old flowers is common advice, but I also clip back the nonblooming stems and have been known to chop off errant limbs entirely in a summer fit. If you grow *B. davidii*, the more popular butterfly bush, cut it way back in late fall or early spring each year to promote flowering the next year. But if you grow fountain butterfly bush (*B. alternifolia*), prune hard after flowering.

Q14. *River birch.* I like the way the river birch trees in my front yard look. They are five years old and now someone tells me they don't live very long. Can you tell me if that's true?

A14. The big problem with river birch is that after about ten years of age they mature rapidly and begin to drop twigs and limbs. Still, there's no better fast-growing tree for uplifting form, fine-textured leaves, and that gorgeous peeling bark. Keep it pest free in the summer, prune it each winter to keep it neat, and fertilize just before new growth starts in spring for longest life.

Q15. *Lots of lantana.* The lantana in my side garden bed is huge and starting to block other plants; it doesn't look so great, either. Should I cut it back, or is it too late?

A15. Rejuvenating plants like lantana and impatiens at midsummer is one of the great joys of a long growing season. Cut back everything that looks ragged, then shape what's left. If any of the stems you've cut off look good, try rooting them in water or soil. You may not want any more, but a neighbor probably does.

Q16. *Leftover chemicals.* I seem to have moved in after some real gardeners, and have questions about some of the stuff they left behind. Should I use the pesticides in the storage room? I recognize some, like malathion, but I've never heard of thiodan. I also found what looks like a shower head that can screw on to the water hose, and there are yellow things hanging in some of the trees. What are these things?

A16. They may have worked in the yard, but those folks weren't true gardeners or good citizens, either, or those chemicals would have been disposed of properly before you moved in. Don't use any of them. You don't know their age or condition. Locate a toxic waste disposal site or program in your area. Sounds like they left you one of my treasures, a water breaker. Every nozzle is designed to break the stream of water into droplets that rain gently instead of beat down on your plants. Clean it with a bleach solution and use it regularly. The yellow things are probably insect traps, sticky bars that allow you to monitor the insect population. That's important so you can identify problems, recognize beneficial bugs, and take steps when needed to protect your plants.

Q17. *Bleach on geraniums.* I love geraniums and have found that I can keep them going for several years at a time by growing them on the north side of my house in pots during the summer. But I forgot to move them when I had the house washed, and the leaves are spotted. Is this from the bleach?

A17. Probably. Geranium leaves are thick and hairy, so it's hard for them to shed toxic substances like bleach. I'd pick the affected leaves off, then cut back what's left so it doesn't look ragged. Fertilize with a soluble flower formula that you mix in water so if they survive they can put on new leaves and flowers. Congratulations on growing geraniums through the summer—that's their most difficult season.

Q18. *When to prune gardenias.* When can I prune gardenias? They bloom fine, but the bushes are too big and seem to have more leaves on some branches than others.

A18. It is best to wait a bit to see how they look this year. Then, after the flowers have finished, shape them right away so they can put on new growth and buds for next year. Thin out the parts that are denser, cut out any dead or twiggy wood, and fertilize with a formula designed for acid-loving shrubs like azaleas, camellias, gardenias, and hollies.

Q19. *Dreadful dodder.*

Last year a vine took over one of my beds and I want to know what to do to prevent it this year. It's thin and I can't see any leaves on it at all, but it's yellow and orange and it has spread all over the bed. What is this?

A19.

It sounds like you had a terrible vine called dodder (*Cuscuta* species) in your garden last year. It's an annual, parasitic weed that looks like somebody blasted the plants with a can of orange silly string. Dodder is leafless, but does bloom, usually in late fall to reseed itself for the next year. The best way to get rid of it is to rip it out at first sight, and even to remove the plants it has infested. A thick layer of mulch in the bed will slow down new seedlings of dodder the next spring.

Q20. *Dividing hostas and holly ferns.*

My aunt wants to share her hostas and holly ferns with me. Can I dig and divide them now?

A20.

So long as the summer perennials like hosta haven't really taken off yet, spring's a fine time to divide them. If the plants are already up and growing actively, wait until fall. Holly fern (*Circomium falcatum*) is a different matter. Dig and divide right away, replant in soil that's been amended with organic matter, and keep them well-watered until they get re-established in about a month. If you are using the ferns under established trees, be sure to water often and amply all summer.

Q21. *Dead magnolia limbs.*

We just bought a house and noticed there are a few very dead limbs in the magnolia tree out front. Can we prune those now, or should we wait until winter?

A21.

It's always good to prune out dead limbs any time of year, and it's especially important if they present a hazard. Remove the damaged areas, and try to make the last cut a few inches behind the damage in good wood. Slant the cuts so water can shed from the cut stems and do not use pruning paint or anything else to seal them. That old method actually seals in the opportunistic pathogens that can attack healthy tissue.

Q22. *Large, leafless corn plant.* What can I do with a corn plant that is nine feet tall, but only has a few leaves? I want to cut it back, but can I root the part I cut off and will the bottom resprout?

A22. You can make at least two plants and probably more from that *Dracaena fragrans* 'Massangeana'. Don't cut the stem off. Instead, make an 'air layer' by making a small cut in it about six inches down from the leafy area. Use wet sphagnum moss to make a fist-sized lump to cover and surround the cut. Cover the moss with plastic wrap and secure it top and bottom with twist ties (not rubber bands or wire that could cut through the stem). Continue watering and feeding the pot and watch for roots to appear in the plastic. Then cut off the stem below the new roots and pot up the new plant. Now look at what's left. If you have several feet of cane, cut the plant down to about one foot tall. That mother plant should resprout and you can then cut the cane into four-inch long pieces and root those, too, in a mixture of ground bark, sand, and compost.

Q23. *Crowd of hummingbirds.* I have six hummingbird feeders and have had hundreds of hummingbirds in the last few years. But this year there are three or four who fight all the time for one feeder. Is this normal, and what should I do about it?

A23. Enjoy the brouhaha! So long as you're keeping the feeders clean and full (and by late spring that can mean tending them daily) the hummers will pick their favorites and 'fight' for dominance. I hope you've included plants that they love, too, so they have plenty of choices, especially perennial salvias, cupheas, and glory bower.

Q24. *Cramped irises.* My iris bed is six years old and overcrowded. Can I dig and divide it now, and what kind of fertilizer can I use now?

A24. The rule of thumb is to divide perennials in the season opposite their bloom, but your situation is one I've faced by breaking that rule. Working with spring bloomers in fall and vice versa usually retains their natural bloom cycle, but crowded plants fight one another for space, light, and nutrients, and usually deliver few flowers anyway. I'd go ahead with digging and dividing, and replant immediately into the new or reworked bed (or pots if you've got some to swap and share). I fertilize iris in early spring and again after flowering with a granular flower formula

fertilizer with a slow release feature. Find one that is good for three months and is released to the plants when watered or by soil temperature. Use it as soon as you've replanted your divisions.

Q25. *To pot or plant an oakleaf hydrangea.* Someone gave me an oakleaf hydrangea she dug up last winter and put in a pot. Can I plant it now or should I leave it in the pot until fall?

A25. Although fall is the very best time to plant shrubs, I'd let the hydrangea be my guide. If its leaves are intact, good green in color, and the plant sits well in the pot, leave it be. If the plant is obviously stressed—too big for the pot, skimpy growth or none at all—plant it today and coddle it through the hot weather. Water, mulch, provide shade if it wilts every day, and prune off any damaged stems. The oakleaf is a slow grower, but worth the trouble for the flowers.

Q26. *Weak rose stems.* I grow roses to cut for my table, but I've noticed this year some of the stems are weak. I use rose fertilizer on them, prune in February, and need to know if epsom salts will help. If it will, how do I use it—put it in the ground or spray the plants?

A26. Weak stems can signal an overabundance of nitrogen in your fertilizer plan, so use a balanced formula on the roses. But rosarians swear by one third cup epsom salts (magnesium sulfate) sprinkled around each rose once or twice a year. Water in well, and if you get the same results as others, you will see more intense flower colors and more plentiful and stronger canes.

Q27. *Lackluster lamb's ear leaves.* I love lambs' ears and have had a plant for several years. Now it's blooming and I notice the leaves under the flowers aren't looking so good. What can I do?

A27. It takes a happy lamb to bloom, but the effort of blooming does deplete the plant's energy. Cut the flowers and enjoy them in an arrangement—they'll last for about a week. Heavy rain can pound the leaves as you describe, too, but all you need to do is clip off the damaged leaves and rake out the mulch if it's keeping them too wet. Fertilize afterward if you haven't already done so. Use a balanced formula of perennial food, preferably with a slow-release nitrogen source included.

Q28. *Floppy elephant ears.* The elephant ears I planted in a pot are growing great except that they flop over nearly every day. I think the

leaves look a bit pale, too. I water every morning, but by the time I get home, they look awful and I have to water again. What can I do?

A28. Even if it takes a hand truck, move the pot into less sunlight. Obviously, your plant cannot work hard enough to stand the conditions. It's using all the water available each day trying to keep up with its fast growth. Slow it down by limiting light, but don't overwater when you do! A dose of liquid fertilizer probably wouldn't hurt, either.

Q29. *Miserable marigolds.* Why can't I grow marigolds? I plant them when they're small each spring, but by Independence Day they look burned up. I deadhead and fertilize, water and pray, but still they die.

A29. You are not alone. Marigolds look as great to spider mites as they do to us, and most of them weren't bred for summers as hot as ours, either. Plant again next year, but keep the plants watered and fertilized — mites prefer dry, unattended conditions—and wash the leaves to further discourage their efforts. Pick a site that's not in full, blasting sun despite what it says on the tag that comes in dwarf marigolds. For big marigolds that are more heat tolerant, grow the African types.

Q30. *Not so vibrant vincas.* The vincas I planted in May look great, but my neighbor's don't and she wants me to tell her what to do. The only difference I can see is that I planted bigger plants, already with flowers on them, and she planted smaller plants. Hers never have branched and have one stem and only one flower on each one. Can you help?

A30. You've actually answered your own question: you planted bigger plants, so your job is one of maintenance, while the neighbor needs to grow hers more aggressively to get the most out of them. Tell her to cut a few inches off each plant (she should have removed the first flowers right away) to encourage branching, then begin watering regularly and fertilizing with a flower boosting formula mixed in the water about every ten days. Then don't get jealous when hers take off just as yours begin to demand more attention to keep up!

Q31. *Pepper problems.* I grow great hot peppers, but never have gotten a good crop of bell peppers. The green bell peppers are small and not very numerous while the serranos, cayennes, and chili peppers make dozens on each branch. What can I do?

A31. First you need to understand that bell peppers need about twice as much fertilizer as their hot friends to make great peppers. In between the times you fertilize them now, give the bells an extra shot. Mulch seems to be more important to bells. They just don't swell up to their potential if water is ample one day and gone the next. Drought keeps the flowers from setting fruit, too.

Q32. *Lacy leaves.* Something is chewing on the plants—hostas mostly—in my shade garden. There are leaves with ragged edges and holes, and some whole leaves are gone. What pests can be doing this? I don't see anything when I look at the plants. How do I get rid of them?

A32. From your description, the only things I can rule out are small, piercing and sucking insects like aphids, scale, and whiteflies. Beetles can chew neat holes, but you'd probably see them. Deer might eat whole leaves, but they'd leave hoofprints. Slugs and snails will leave slime trails in their wake. But I'm thinking your culprit is some kind of chewing larvae. Many caterpillars have the right size mouthparts to do the damage you describe and would likely be underneath the plants as you observe them. Turn the leaves over, scratch around under the plants, and if you see the culprits, treat only the affected plants with dipel (a naturally occurring predator made into a dust) or rotenone (a reliable control made from the cube plant). Dipel works slowly, but thoroughly; rotenone is a faster control. I prefer either to the traditional carbaryl products.

Q33. *Asiatic jasmine.* For two years I have been trying to get Asiatic jasmine to fill in on a slope outside my porch. I water it and put fertilizer out there, but the weeds keep coming and the jasmine doesn't. Any advice for me?

A33. Yes. The trouble here is you're not growing the jasmine fast enough to beat the weeds. Pull them all out one mo' time, then put a soaker hose or sprinkler in there if you don't have one, add a layer of compost and/or fertilizer around each plant, and mulch two inches deep around every plant. Keep the bed watered—twice a week won't be too much right now—and use a hose-end sprayer to provide additional fertilizer once a month all summer. If the plants still don't outgrow the weeds, go in between each clump this fall and plant more of the jasmine.

Q34. *Triangular bugs!* I see triangular-shaped green bugs on my plants, especially the tomatoes. I see another bug that has the same shape but is brown and kind of spiny. Is the green one a younger version of the brown one and do they eat plants?

A34. No, they're aren't and yes, they do! The smooth skinned ones are bad news whether green or any other color, and the spiny ones are great to have around. The nonspined ones 'sting' tomatoes and inject them with a toxin that really messes up their ripening. Fortunately, some of the spined ones (called predaceous stinkers) eat the bad guys. Identify yours and proceed accordingly. Major infestations usually appear late in the season on tomatoes, and I'd rather dump the plants, remove the debris, and replant for fall. Stinkbugs are another reason to clean up the garden year in fall or winter. Piles of weeds or spent annual flowers and vegetables can harbor many pests.

Q35. *Why roly-polies roll.* We seem to have an invasion of roly-polies in the garden this year. Do they eat plants, and what makes them roll up when you poke them? How do you get rid of them?

A35. They roll up for the same reason people curl up when someone snatches the bedcovers off to wake them up—it's a self-preservation instinct. I don't get rid of them, since both the roly-polies

(*Armadillium vulgare*) and their cousins who don't roll up, the sowbugs (*Procellio* species) spend their nights foraging in the garden. These crustaceans eat rotten plant matter, digest it, and turn it into humus. If there are too many in one part of the garden, it's because the area stays very damp: these guys' favorite daytime sleeping conditions. Scoop up some and relocate them to a drier area where they aren't entrenched, then mulch it to create favorable conditions.

Q36. *Lifeless lawn.* I just bought a home and the lawn looks terrible. At least one fourth of it is brown no matter how much I water it. The neighbor says it's chinchbugs—should I believe him?

A36. Slow down just a minute and make sure chinchbug (*Blissus insularis*) is your pest. The damage starts as small yellow patches that turn brown and eventually run together into big dead zones. The dry brown grass just peels off when you grab it, unlike where fungus diseases are present—they usually don't detach from the roots. Chinchbugs are no more than 1/6-inches long when mature, so use a hand lens to look for them (usually you'll see the red bodies with a lighter band across their back of the younger bugs. The adults are black and almost invisible, but do move away when you part the grass). Or cut both ends off a coffee can, sink it three inches into your turf, and fill it with water. The chinchbugs will float up to the surface so you can identify them. If you also see what looks like chinchbugs with big eyes, count your blessings. They are predators and can help control the problem in the long run. However, many of them will also be killed by chemical treatments for a serious problem with chinchbugs.

To prevent reinfestation, keep the lawn watered regularly and use a balanced fertilizer-too much nitrogen alone actually increases the bugs' chances. And, yes, you will probably have to replant the dead lawn areas. Look for a resistant variety of St. Augustine or choose another, less vulnerable turf.

Q37. *Ants and aphids.* I have heard that ants harvest aphids. Do they eat them or what?

A37. Ants do 'farm' aphids. They tote them around and eat the honeydew the aphids put out. But I disagree with the authorities who tell us this is always a bad thing. The ants will actually move the aphids to a preferred plant and guard them from other predators. My positive experience has to do with okra. The aphid population does not seem to

increase rapidly when the ants are tending them on my okra. Each time I've had this biorelationship going, the other vegetable plants have had no aphids at all, and as long as I picked the okra regularly, it didn't seem affected. I do recommend controlling ants in the garden area, but more to protect against the stings of fire ants and to avoid the annoyance of black 'sweet' ants.

Q38. *Sticky trees.* My mother's plum trees are always gorgeous and full of fruit, but this year they're wilting and the crape myrtles have weird white stuff sticking out of the trunk near the bottom. It looks like a little toothpick but isn't sticky. What is it, and will it hurt the trees?

A38. The name sounds goofy, but it's likely both trees and perhaps other hardwoods in the area are infested with Asian ambrosia beetles (*Xylosandrus crassiusculus*). The stuff you're seeing is left by the mama beetle as she drills a place to lay eggs inside the tree. Then she tends a fungus called ambrosia inside her nest to feed her young, who grow up inside the tree, then mate and emerge to infest another tree. I'm very sorry, but you will have to cut down the infested trees, then prevent damage to the healthy ones. Keep the trees watered and fertilized, avoid wounding them with mowers or trimmers, prune only during the dormant season, and spray the healthy trunks with a contact insecticide labeled for beetles in March each year. Monitor the trees carefully.

Q39. *Worm attack on azaleas!* When I looked at my azaleas this morning, they were crawling with striped worms that had big orange ends on them, so I grabbed some malathion and sprayed them. Some of them fell off, but what are they and what else do I need to do to get rid of them?

A39. This morning, you had a bird's-eye-view of azalea caterpillars (*Datana major*). Did you notice that their undersides are almost white but their legs are orange, too? They've been there since spring when their mama moth laid eggs. If you noticed a few leaves that had only their veins left, you know when the larvae began feeding. Once they get big enough, they can strip an azalea completely. Fortunately, it seldom kills the shrub, but losing all its leaves every year does take its toll. Malathion is a contact insecticide—that means it kills nearly every bug it touches, including the beneficial insects in your garden. I applaud your targeted use of the product for this specific outbreak, but for long term control, use Thuricide or Dipel. It's made from *Bacillus thuringiensis kurstaki,* a microscopic critter that eats

butterfly and moth larvae for lunch. Be sure to rake out and discard old leaves and mulch under the shrubs this fall. Replace with fresh mulch to prevent overwintering of the insects.

Q40. *Spotty beetles.* There are beetles with spots on their backs eating my roses and the same bug is all over my cucumbers. What are they, and how can I control them? I won't have any leaves left if this keeps up.

A40. They are aptly named: spotted cucumber beetles (*Diabrotica acalymna vittata*) build up their populations on a variety of host plants, laying eggs in the soil, hatching larvae to eat roots, emerging to attack leaves, stems, and even flowers. There's also a striped 'cousin' beetle who eats just vegetables, but the spotted one likes lots of plants. Sometimes an even bigger problem results when the beetles bring in virus diseases to vegetable plants. When only a few beetles are present, it's actually fun to pluck them off with tweezers and drop them into a cup of bleach, but to save a crop from destruction, use a rotenone or carbaryl (Sevin) dust or a pyrethrin spray. When using any product on an edible plant, always read the label and observe the waiting time before harvesting.

Q41. *Kinds of tomatoes.*
What's the difference between spring tomatoes and fall tomatoes? Are there different varieties for each time, or do you grow them differently?

A41. Other than watering and fertilizing a bit more to get the 'fall' tomatoes through the heat of July and August, the only difference in the tomatoes is in their heat tolerance. Most often you'll see fewer varieties for sale as the fall crop, and they'll have names like 'SolarSet' that reveal their forte. But traditional southern favorite tomatoes ('Better Boy', 'Sweet 100', and 'Roma') make a fine fall crop. If you can keep the spring vines healthy, they'll begin bearing sooner than plants started in July.

Q42. *Mimosas and more old garden trees.* The house I bought has an old garden that includes tallow trees, mimosa, and lots of oxalis and cast iron plants. My granddaughter wants to start some of them. Are any of these worth having?

A42. Except for the tallow tree (*Sapium schiferum*), I'd say you have classic southern plants that deserve attention. The tallow (or popcorn) tree is such an invader that it is banned in parts of our region. Yet its fall color is glorious where so few trees really show off, and the seedpods (the popcorn) are a staple of autumn decorating! The mimosa is making a comeback despite its reputation as a short-lived litterer. Who cares? Every child loves to 'powder' their face with the flower, the fragrance is very pleasant, and the tree grows fast. Have your granddaughter dig a seedling next spring to transplant right away. Oxalis (pink or yellow) and the classic aspidistra (cast iron plant) grow well in sun, but are especially desirable because they tolerate shade. Dig and divide their clumps in late winter, and pass on your loving legacy.

Nellie Neal

Nellie Neal answers questions from real gardeners every day. They seek out her smarts in the grocery store checkout line, at school events, and once (but only once) in the ladies' room at a concert. Known as the GardenMama on her weekly radio program, she fields callers' queries about every aspect of their mutual passion.

The GardenMama is a southern gardener, garden writer, talk radio host, lecturer, wife, and mother. She grew her first begonia in third grade, zinnias in coffee cans on a California fire escape, and 99 tomato plants in the front yard one summer. She knows how to make plants grow, and practices what she preaches. Her tried-and-true garden practices are wisely adapted to twenty-first century concerns of time, space, and environmental awareness.

Nellie Neal writes and speaks from a solid educational background coupled with a lifetime of gardening successes and failures. She learned to garden from her grandfather, and went on to major in English and Horticulture at LSU in Baton Rouge (B.S., 1975). Her expertise in general horticulture subjects is based on experience across the Southeast in USDA Zones 7, 8, and 9 plus the coastal areas of California. She has more than

twenty-five years' experience in both the businesses and pleasures of the field. She has grown plants, bought and sold plants, tested new varieties, and helped sustain old ones. She has planted and maintained landscapes and movie sets, mowed lawns, watered greenhouses, waited on customers in garden retail, and taught gardening to students of every age. Nellie has spent time with Master Gardeners, Girl Scouts and third graders, adults who consult her, youth diversion program offenders, people with disabilities, garden club ladies, professional horticulture practitioners, plant society members, and a host of neighbors, and has learned valuable lessons from them all. Today she gardens mostly in Mississippi and Louisiana and has never met a plant she didn't like.

111

Nellie was co-publisher of Loose Dirt newsletter and co-wrote *The Garden Primer for the Deep South*, was Horticulture Editor for *Mississippi Gardens* magazine, and contributed to *Rodale's Low Maintenance Gardening, Annuals for Dummies*, and *eHow.com*. She wrote a column for *Rebecca's Garden* magazine, and served as Contributing Editor for Ortho's *All About Greenhouses*.

These days, she writes for regional magazines including *Louisiana Gardener* and *Mississippi* Gardener, *The Gardener's Companion* newsletter, state and national newspapers, and the internet, including *nationalgardening.com* and her website, *www.gardenmama.com*. She has been a member of the Garden Writers Association of America since 1992 and served as its Awards Committee Chairperson in 1998. Now folks take notes when she speaks, and make two frequent observations about the GardenMama: she makes the science of gardening easily understood, and her reality-based advice works!

Recommended Reading

There is no required reading in gardening. Lots of people learn all they need to know by watching others and asking questions, by trial and error, or plain good luck. But as an avid reader of everything from cereal boxes to Hortus Third, I know the value of a great book. To make my list, a resource must offer proven information in an easily readable style with illustrations that add to the text in practical ways. Some are broad-based collections of information, others are plant specific; all have given me comfort. And I assure you, these selections are not insomnia cures!

Dirr's Trees and Shrubs for Warm Climates, Michael A. Dirr, Timber Press, Portland, OR, 2002. At last, an encyclopedia you can read without a dictionary close at hand, Dr. Dirr starts with his personal garden and takes you across the region with brilliant descriptions and his own photos.

Passalong Plants, Steve Bender and Felder Rushing, UNC Press, Chapel Hill, NC, 1993. This collection of vignettes puts names on the venerable cottage garden plants you seldom see in the trade, but always find in someone's garden. A scream of a read—put this award-winner in your bathroom.

Gardening in the Humid South, Edmund N. O'Rourke, Jr., and Leon C. Standifer, LSU Press, Baton Rouge, LA, 2002. My major professor in graduate school and the toughest seminar prof I ever had have joined forces to explain horticulture to us all. It's like reading a boxing match—each punch from one is met by a jab from the other. Like them, an inspiration.

Southern Herb Growing, Madelyn Hill and Gwen Barclay, Shearer Publishing, Fredericksburg, TX, 1987. Let this mother-daughter team expand your definition of 'herbs' to include perennials you never thought of, and learn to bake the best Rose Geranium cake ever eaten.

Bulletproof Flowers for the South, Jim Wilson, Taylor Publishing Co., Dallas, TX, 1999. If you agree the best test of a flower is how soon it recovers from pounding thunderstorms, you'll understand the reason for this book. Anything Jim writes is worth reading.

Jim Wilson's Container Gardening, Taylor Trade Publishing, Dallas, TX, 2000. The future of gardening sits right on your deck—no tilling, no digging, but pounds of tomatoes, beautiful flowering combinations, and great advice for novice and veteran gardeners—see comment above.

Commonsense Vegetable Gardening for the South, William D. Adams and Thomas LeRoy, Taylor Publishing Co., Dallas, TX, 1995. Though I never agree a hundred percent with anyone on vegetable gardening, these guys cover nearly all the bases with emphasis on cultural practices over chemical controls.

Native Shrubs and Vines for the Southeast, Leonard Foote and Samuel B. Jones, Jr., Timber Press, Portland, OR, 1989. More than 500 shrubs and vines are included and most of them should be used more in landscapes around the region.

Gardening 'Round Atlanta, Avis Y. Aronovitz, Eldorado Publishers, Atlanta, GA, 1996. Real world advice that applies to areas well beyond Hotlanta—nobody else ever told me to use a brown paper bag to shade new transplants in hot or cold weather.

Creative Propagation: a Grower's Guide, Peter Thompson, Timber Press, Portland, OR, 1989, 1992. When you get serious about taking cuttings of every plant you have, refer to this book to know when and how to have the best success.

Garden Flowers from Seed, Christopher Lloyd and Graham Rice, Timber Press, Portland, OR, 1994. A classic reprinted in accessible paperback, with vast information unavailable elsewhere about specific flower seed-starting techniques.

A Cutting Garden for Florida, Betty Barr Mackey and Monica Moran Brandies, B. B. Mackey Books, Wayne, PA, 3rd edition, 2001. Newly updated and expanded with an excellent selection of plants and how to beat heat and humidity to grow them.

Southern Living Garden Book, Steve Bender, Editor, Oxmoor House, Birmingham, AL, 1998. A long-awaited basic tome, written with attention to detail and clear explanations of the zone descriptions within our region.

Southern Living Garden Problem Solver, Steve Bender, Editor, Oxmoor House, Birmingham, AL, 1999. Ideas for curing many garden ills common across the South, with pictures you hope never to see in your own garden.

Annuals for Dummies, Bill Marken (Nellie Neal, Regional Contributor), IDG Books, 1998. Despite the name, this series of books has much to offer in basic information, broad based and very mainstream.

Ortho's All About Greenhouses, Nellie Neal (Contributing Editor), Meredith Publishing, Des Moines, IA, 2001. It was my pleasure to work on the latest edition of the best-selling Ortho book ever and I recommend it to those considering or already addicted to greenhouse growing.

The New Orleans Garden, Charlotte Seidenberg, University Press of MS, Jackson, MS, 1990, 1993. Invaluable for those in coastal areas and written with the grace of a southern breeze, you'll learn as much about plants and culture as New Orleans gardening landmarks.

Insects and Gardens, Eric Grissell, Timber Press, Portland, OR, 2001. I've waited years for someone to explain the dynamics of horticultural entomology in real world terms and this book comes as close as Timber's *Botany for Gardeners* does on that subject.

Attracting Birds to Southern Gardens, Thomas Pope, Neil Odenwald, Charles Fryling, Jr., Taylor Publishing Co., 1993. Until these guys took it on, nobody had written about landscaping for birding—they did it well.

Attracting Butterflies and Hummingbirds to your Garden, Sally Roth, Rodale Press, Emmaus, PA, 2001. A newer book, this one genuinely transfers the writer's joy and expertise to the reader.

Encyclopedia of Organic Gardening, J. I. Rodale and Staff, Editors, Rodale Press, Emmaus, PA, 1959, 1999.

Roses in the Southern Garden, G. Michael Shoup, Antique Rose Emporium, Brenham, TX, 2000. Yes, this is written by the owner of the Emporium, a passionate rosarian with great experience rediscovering and expanding the genera. Well-written and extensive in its scope.

Armitage's Garden Perennials, Allan M. Armitage, Timber Press, Portland, OR, 2000. A tireless plantsman and hort professor (U of GA in Athens) provides the lowdown and photographs of hundreds of perennials suited to the South.

The Southern Gardener's Book of Lists, Lois Trigg Chaplin, Taylor Publishing Co., Dallas, TX, 1994. An astounding collection of plant choices for every situation you can imagine. Having the lists can lead you to group plants that actually grow in the same conditions.

Warm Climate Gardening, Barbara Pleasant, Garden Way Books, Storey Communications, Pownal, VT, 1993. Useful ideas, with cogent explanations of why they work here. Written by an experienced and dedicated author, this book fills a big void in southern gardening information.

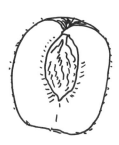

Notes

INDEX

<u>Questions and Answers for Deep South Gardeners</u>